BC SCIENCE 8
Student V

Authors

Briar Ballou
Handsworth Secondary School
North Vancouver, British Columbia

Jon Bocknek
Science Writer
Vallican, British Columbia

Van Chau
Delview Secondary School
Delta, British Columbia

Program Consultants

Sandy Wohl
Hugh Boyd Secondary School
Richmond, British Columbia

Herb Johnston
Faculty of Education
University of British Columbia
Vancouver, British Columbia

Douglas A. Roberts
Professor Emeritus of Education
University of Calgary
Calgary, Alberta

Lionel Sandner
Saanich School District #63
Saanichton, British Columbia

McGraw-Hill Ryerson

Toronto   Montréal   Boston   Burr Ridge, IL   Dubuque, IA
Madison, WI   New York   San Francisco   St. Louis   Bangkok   Bogotá
Caracas   Kuala Lumpur   Lisbon   London   Madrid   Mexico City
Milan   New Delhi   Santiago   Seoul   Singapore   Sydney   Taipei

The McGraw·Hill Companies

Mc Graw Hill **McGraw-Hill Ryerson**

COPIES OF THIS BOOK
MAY BE OBTAINED BY
CONTACTING:
McGraw-Hill Ryerson Ltd.

WEB SITE:
http://www.mcgrawhill.ca

E-MAIL:
orders@mcgrawhill.ca

TOLL-FREE FAX:
1-800-463-5885

TOLL-FREE CALL:
1-800-565-5758

OR BY MAILING YOUR
ORDER TO:
McGraw-Hill Ryerson
Order Department
300 Water Street
Whitby, ON L1N 9B6

Please quote the ISBN and
title when placing your order.

Student Workbook ISBN:
0-07-097296-6

McGraw-Hill Ryerson
BC Science 8 Workbook
Copyright © 2006, McGraw-Hill Ryerson Limited, a Subsidiary of The McGraw-Hill
Companies. All rights reserved. No part of this publication may be reproduced or
transmitted in any form or by any means, or stored in a data base or retrieval system,
without the prior written permission of McGraw-Hill Ryerson Limited, or, in the
case of photocopying or other reprographic copying, a licence from The Canadian
Copyright Licensing Agency (Access Copyright). For an Access Copyright licence,
visit *www.accesscopyright.ca* or call toll free to 1-800-893-5777.

The information and activities in this textbook have been carefully developed and
reviewed by professionals to ensure safety and accuracy. However, the publisher shall
not be liable for any damages resulting, in whole or in part, from the reader's use of
the material. Although appropriate safety procedures are discussed and highlighted
throughout the textbook, the safety of students remains the responsibility of the class-
room teacher, the principal, and the school board district.

ISBN 0-07-097296-6

www.mcgrawhill.ca

1   2   3   4   5   6   7   8   9   10   MP   0   9   8   7   6

Printed and bound in Canada

Care has been taken to trace ownership of copyright material contained in this text.
The publishers will gladly accept any information that will enable them to rectify any
reference or credit in subsequent printings.

SCIENCE PUBLISHER: Keith Owen Richards
DEVELOPMENT HOUSE: Pronk&Associates
DEVELOPMENTAL EDITOR: Tricia Armstrong
COPY EDITOR: Allison Black
MANAGER, EDITORIAL SERVICES: Crystal Shortt
SUPERVISING EDITOR: Jeanette McCurdy
EDITORIAL ASSISTANT: Erin Hartley
MANAGER, PRODUCTION SERVICES: Yolanda Pigden
PRODUCTION COORDINATOR: Sheryl MacAdam
COVER DESIGN: Pronk&Associates/Dianna Little
ART DIRECTION: Brian Lehen Graphic Design Ltd.
ELECTRONIC PAGE MAKE-UP: Brian Lehen Graphic Design Ltd.

Contents

Chapter 3   The immune system protects the human body.

UNIT 2   Optics

Chapter 4   Many properties of light can be understood using a wave model of light.

Chapter 5   Optical systems make use of mirrors and lenses.

UNIT 4   Water Systems on Earth

Chapter 10   The water cycle plays a vital role on Earth.

Observing Living Things

Textbook pages 8–21

Before You Read

This section describes the signs that scientists look for to help them decide if something is living or non-living. On the lines below, list two living things and then list two non-living things.

_____

_____

 Mark the Text

Identify Details

As you skim the section, use one colour to highlight the text or labels that talk about parts of a microscope. Use another colour to highlight facts about microscopes.

How can you tell if something is living or non-living?

All living things have certain characteristics in common. Something is living if it has all of these characteristics:

◆ responds to its environment

◆ needs energy

◆ grows

◆ reproduces

◆ gets rid of wastes that build up in its body

Another name for a living thing is **organism**. All organisms are made up of cells. A cell is the smallest living part of a living thing. Single-celled organisms are called **unicellular**. Organisms made of many cells are called **multicellular**.

How can you see cells?

Most cells are too small to see with just your eyes. You need a microscope to see them. At school you use a **compound light microscope**. It is a compound microscope because it combines two lenses. It is a light microscope because it uses light to view an object. A compound light microscope is shown on the next page.

A microscope helps you focus two objects or details that are close together. This is called **resolving power**. A microscope also makes an object seem larger than it is. This is called **magnification power**. When you look into a microscope, the object you see is magnified, reversed, and turned upside down (inverted). ◉

Reading Check

1. What are two things that a microscope does?

_____

_____

_____

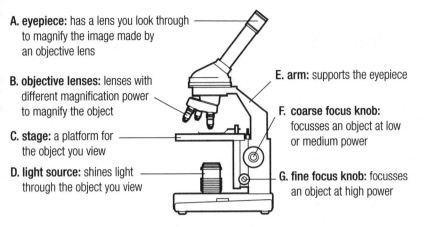

A. **eyepiece:** has a lens you look through to magnify the image made by an objective lens

B. **objective lenses:** lenses with different magnification power to magnify the object

C. **stage:** a platform for the object you view

D. **light source:** shines light through the object you view

E. **arm:** supports the eyepiece

F. **coarse focus knob:** focusses an object at low or medium power

G. **fine focus knob:** focusses an object at high power

The eyepiece lens often has a magnification power of 10×. This means that an object seems ten times larger when you look at it with the lens. Each objective lens has its own power of magnification. The low-power lens is 4×. The medium-power lens is 10×. The high-power lens is 40×.

How large does an object look when you combine the eyepiece lens with each objective lens? Use the table below to find out. ✅

Power of objective lens	Power of eyepiece lens	Calculation (power of objective lens multiplied by power of eyepiece lens)	Total magnification of the lens combination
low power: 4×	10×	4 × 10 = 40	40×
medium power: 10×	10×	10 × 10 = 100	100×
high power: 40×	10×	40 × 10 = 400	400×

Are there stronger types of microscopes?

A light microscope can magnify an object up to 2000×. An electron microscope is much stronger. An electron microscope uses electrons instead of light to make an object look larger. One type of electron microscope is called a **scanning electron microscope**. It can magnify an object up to 200 000×.

A camera or a monitor can be hooked up to an electron microscope. The picture that appears on the camera film or on the screen is called an **electron micrograph**. Many of the pictures in Chapter 1 of *BC Science 8* are electron micrographs.

✔ *Reading Check*

2. How large will an object look if you use a 4× eyepiece lens with a low-power objective lens?

_____

_____

_____

Use with textbook page 11.

Characteristics of living things

List five characteristics of living things. Give an example for each characteristic.

	Characteristic of living things	Example
1.		
2.		
3.		
4.		
5.		

Name   Date

Use with textbook page 12.

The compound light microscope

Identify the following parts of a compound light microscope.

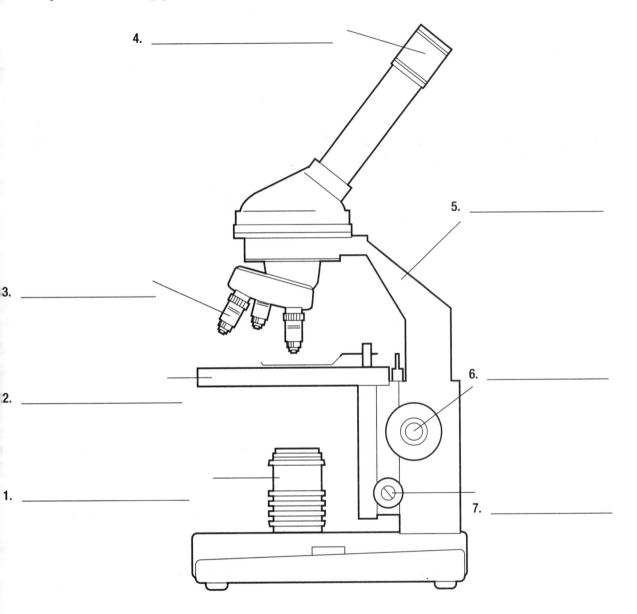

4. _____

5. _____

3. _____

2. _____

6. _____

1. _____

7. _____

Use with textbook pages 11–14.

Microscopes

Vocabulary	
coarse focus knob	magnification power
compound light microscope	objective lenses
electron micrograph	resolving power
eyepiece	reversed
fine focus knob	right side up
light source	upside down

Use the terms in the vocabulary box to fill in the blanks. Use each term only once. You will not need to use all the terms.

1. The _____ is the microscope usually used in science classes and medical laboratories.

2. The _____ is used for viewing and contains a lens that magnifies.

3. The _____ brings an object into focus at low or medium power.

4. The _____ brings an object into focus at high power.

5. The _____ have different magnification power to magnify the object.

6. The _____ supplies the light needed to view the slide.

7. The ability to distinguish between objects that are very close together is called _____ .

8. When you look through a microscope, you will observe an image that is magnified, _____ , and _____ .

9. A(n) _____ is a picture taken by a camera hooked up to an electron microscope.

se with textbook pages 8–21.

Observing living things

Match each Term on the left with the best Descriptor on the right. Each Descriptor may be used only once.

Term	Descriptor
1. _____ compound light microscope	**A.** power of the objective lens multiplied by the power of the eyepiece
2. _____ objective lenses	**B.** has two sets of lenses
3. _____ eyepiece	**C.** used for viewing and magnifying the image
4. _____ stage	**D.** ability to distinguish between two objects that are very close to each other
5. _____ arm	
6. _____ total magnification	**E.** supports the eyepiece
7. _____ resolving power	**F.** have different magnification powers to magnify the object
	G. supports the slide

Circle the letter of the best answer.

8. Which of the following is not a characteristic of living things?

A. needs energy

B. hunts for food

C. grows

D. reproduces

9. What is the difference between a unicellular and a multicellular organism?

A. size of cells

B. structure of cells

C. shape of cells

D. number of cells

10. Which of the following is not a use of a microscope?

A. magnifies distant objects

B. magnifies objects that are close together

C. magnifies unicellular organisms

D. magnifies cells

11. Which of the following best describes an electron micrograph?

A. a type of electron microscope

B. a camera hooked up to an electron microscope

C. a picture shown on a screen hooked up to an electron microscope

D. a scanning electron microscope

12. If the objective lens is 40× and the eyepiece lens is 10×, what is the total magnification?

A. 400×

B. 40×

C. 10×

D. 4×

13. If the objective lens is 10× and the eyepiece lens is 10×, what is the total magnification?

A. 10×

B. 100×

C. 1000×

D. 20×

Cells

Textbook pages 22–39

Before You Read

How might the cells of a plant be like the cells of an animal? How might they be different? Write your ideas in the space below.

Mark the Text

Identify Definitions
Highlight the definition of each word that appears in bold type.

Reading Check

1. How is a prokaryotic cell different from a eukaryotic cell?

_____

_____

_____

What is the cell theory?

The **cell theory** states three important facts about cells.

1. The cell is the basic unit of all life.

2. All living things are made up of one or more cells.

3. All cells come from other living cells.

How are prokaryotic cells different from eukaryotic cells?

There are two main types of cells. **Eukaryotic cells** are cells with organelles that have a membrane around them. You will find out more about organelles below. Plant cells and animal cells are eukaryotic cells.

   Prokaryotic cells are cells that do *not* have organelles with membranes around them. **Bacteria** are prokaryotic cells that live just about everywhere on Earth. Some bacteria cause diseases. ✔

   It is easy to confuse bacteria with another type of tiny thing that causes disease: viruses. **Viruses** are non-living things that are able to reproduce. Viruses are not cells. Viruses must be present inside the cell of a living thing in order to reproduce.

What is inside a cell?

All cells have **organelles** that carry out specific tasks that help the cell to survive. Most of the organelles in animal cells are also found in plant cells. However, animal cells do not have a cell wall or chloroplasts.

Typical Cell Structures

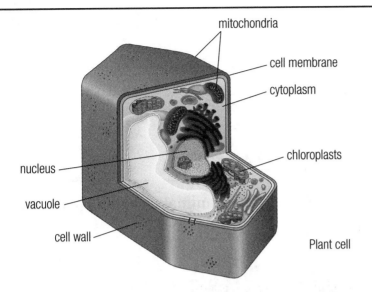

mitochondria

cell membrane

cytoplasm

chloroplasts

nucleus

vacuole

cell wall

Plant cell

cell membrane: This structure is like a skin that surrounds the whole cell. The cell membrane keeps the inside of the cell separate from what is outside it. The cell membrane also controls what enters and leaves the cell.

nucleus: The nucleus of the cell controls all the cell's activities.

cytoplasm: This clear, jelly-like fluid holds the organelles of the cell in place.

mitochondria: These bean-shaped structures are the energy producers.

vacuoles: Vacuoles store materials such as wastes for a short time. Plant cells usually have one large vacuole. Animal cells have many small vacuoles.

cell wall: The cell wall surrounds the cell membrane of plant cells. The cell wall gives the plant cell protection and supports its box-like shape.

chloroplasts: These green-coloured structures in plant cells trap the Sun's light energy and change it to chemical energy for use by the cell.

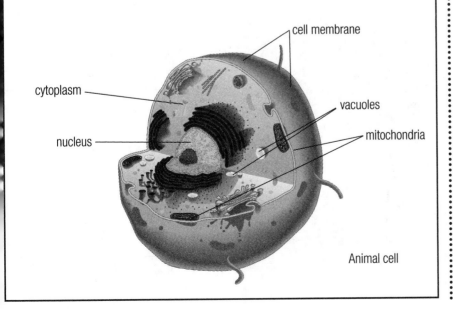

cell membrane

cytoplasm

vacuoles

nucleus

mitochondria

Animal cell

Reading Check

2. Name two organelles that are found in plant cells but not in animal cells.

_____

_____

Use with textbook page 27.

Parts of cells

Vocabulary	
cell membrane	vacuole
nucleus	vacuoles
cell wall	cytoplasm
chloroplast	mitochondria

Use the terms in the box to label the parts of an animal cell and a plant cell. Terms may be used more than once.

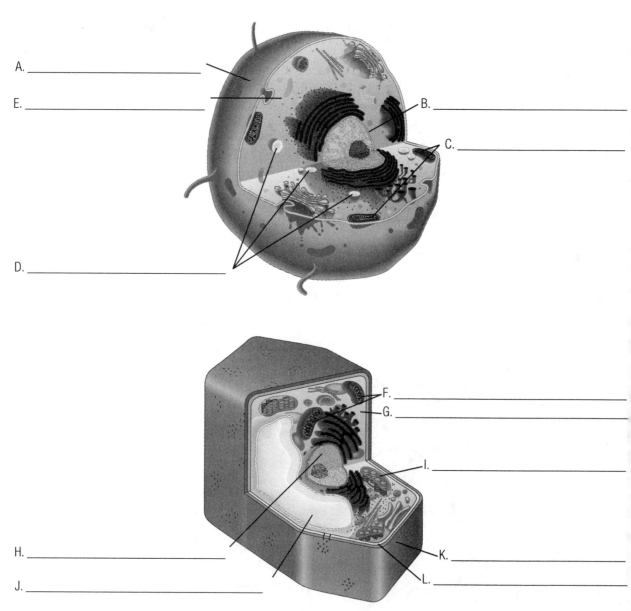

A. _____

E. _____

B. _____

C. _____

D. _____

F. _____

G. _____

I. _____

H. _____

K. _____

J. _____

L. _____

Use with textbook pages 24–29.

Inside a cell

Vocabulary	
bacteria	living thing
cell theory	mitochondria
cell membrane	organelle
cell wall	prokaryotic
chloroplasts	nucleus
cytoplasm	vacuoles
eukaryotic	viruses

Use the terms in the vocabulary box to fill in the blanks. Each term may be used only once. You will not need to use all the terms.

1. A(n) _____ is a cell structure in which functions are carried out to ensure the cell's survival.

2. Each cell is surrounded by a _____ that separates the interior of the cell from its surroundings.

3. Within the cell is a jelly-like substance called _____.

4. The _____ is the organelle that controls all the activities within the cell.

5. The _____ are the energy producers in the cell.

6. _____ are temporary storage compartments that sometimes store waste.

7. The _____ is a tough, rigid structure that surrounds the cell membrane and protects the cell.

8. The _____ trap the energy from the Sun and change it into chemical energy.

9. Plant and animal cells are examples of _____ cells.

10. _____ cells are cells that do not have organelles with membranes around them.

11. _____ are examples of prokaryotic cells that can cause disease.

12. _____ are examples of non-living things that are able to reproduce.

Use with textbook pages 32–34.

True or false?

Read the statements given below. If the statement is true, write "T" on the line in front of the statement. If it is false, write "F" and rewrite the statement to make it true.

1. _____ The cell is the basic unit of life.

_____

_____

2. _____ All organisms are composed of only one cell.

_____

_____

3. _____ Animal cells use chloroplasts to trap the Sun's energy.

_____

_____

4. _____ Prokaryotic cells are cells that are surrounded by a cell wall.

_____

_____

5. _____ Eukaryotic cells are cells that are surrounded by a cell membrane.

_____

_____

6. _____ Some bacteria cause diseases.

_____

_____

7. _____ Viruses are non-living things.

_____

_____

8. _____ Bacteria are an example of eukaryotic cells.

_____

_____

Use with textbook pages 22–39.

Cells

Circle the letter of the best answer.

1. Cell membranes are found in

   A. plant cells only

   B. animal cells only

   C. neither plant or animal cells

   D. both plant and animal cells

2. Which comparison between plant and animal cells is correct?

	Plants	Animals
A.	no chloroplasts	chloroplasts
B.	no mitochondria	mitochondria
C.	nucleus	no nucleus
D.	cell wall	no cell wall

3. Which of the following describes the cell theory?

I.	The cell is the basic unit of life.
II.	All organisms are composed of one or more cells.
III.	Two or more cells are necessary to produce new cells.
IV.	All cells come from other living cells.

   A. I, II, and III only

   B. I, II, and IV only

   C. I, III, and IV only

   D. II, III, and IV only

4. Which of the following statements is true?

   A. A eukaryotic cell has organelles surrounded by membranes.

   B. A prokaryotic cell has organelles surrounded by membranes.

   C. All eukaryotic cells are surrounded by a cell wall.

   D. All prokaryotic cells are surrounded by a cell wall.

5. Bacteria are examples of

   A. organelles

   B. viruses

   C. prokaryotic cells

   D. eukaryotic cells

6. Plant cells are examples of

   A. organelles

   B. bacteria

   C. prokaryotic cells

   D. eukaryotic cells

Match each Term on the left with the best Descriptor on the right. Each Descriptor may be used only once.	
Term	**Descriptor**
7. _____ cell membrane 8. _____ nucleus 9. _____ cytoplasm 10. _____ mitochondria 11. _____ vacuoles 12. _____ cell wall 13. _____ chloroplasts	**A.** produces energy **B.** controls all the cell's activities **C.** protects and supports plant cells **D.** traps light energy **E.** stores materials such as wastes **F.** controls what enters and leaves a cell **G.** organelles without a membrane around them **H.** holds the organelles in place

Section

1.3
Summary

Diffusion, Osmosis, and the Cell Membrane

Textbook pages 40–49

Before You Read

In this section you will learn about two ways in which some substances can move into a cell and out of a cell through its membrane. On the lines below, list two things that you think should be able to move into a cell. Then list two things that should not be able to move into a cell. Think of things a cell might need and things that might harm a cell.

Create a Quiz

After you have read this section, create a five-question quiz based on what you have learned. After you have written the questions, be sure to answer them.

Reading Check

1. In what two ways does diffusion help cells?

_____

_____

What is the cell membrane like?

The cell membrane is a **selectively permeable membrane**. This means that it has many small openings that let some substances pass through it but not others. You can picture the membrane like a window screen in your home that lets air pass through it but keeps insects out. Substances that are smaller than the openings in a cell membrane can move into the cell from outside it. Substances that are larger than the openings cannot move into the cell.

How does diffusion move substances through the cell membrane?

One way that substances can move through the cell membrane is by diffusion. **Diffusion** happens when particles move from a place where there are more of them into a place where there are fewer of them.

    Concentration is the amount of a substance in a certain place. A place that has a higher concentration of particles in it has more particles than a place that has a lower concentration.

    Diffusion moves substances that a cell needs from outside the cell to inside the cell. This is how the oxygen that most cells need moves into a cell. Diffusion also moves wastes from inside the cell to outside the cell. This is how carbon dioxide, a waste gas in some cells, moves out of a cell. ✔

Name

Date

Section

1.3

Summary

continued

How does osmosis move substances through the cell membrane?

Osmosis is a special kind of diffusion that involves water. **Osmosis** is the diffusion of water through a selectively permeable membrane. Osmosis happens when water particles move from a place where their concentration is higher to a place where their concentration is lower.

Osmosis is important to cells. Cells contain water and need it to survive. Cells also live in water or in watery surroundings. What will happen if the concentration of water inside a cell is higher than outside a cell? Water will move out of the cell by osmosis. What will happen if the concentration of water inside a cell is lower than outside a cell? Water will move into the cell by osmosis. ✔

In A, the rate at which water particles move into the cell is the same as the rate at which they move out of the cell. A plant cell, shown in B, is normal and healthy.

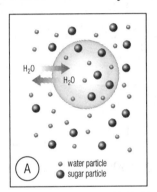

A
• water particle
● sugar particle

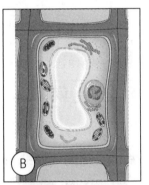

B

In C, the concentration of water particles outside of the cell is higher than inside the cell. Water particles move into the cell by osmosis. A plant cell, shown in D, is swollen with extra water.

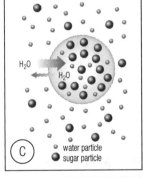

C
• water particle
● sugar particle

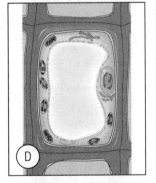

D

In E, the concentration of water particles outside of the cell is lower than inside the cell. Water particles move out of the cell by osmosis. A plant cell, shown in F, loses water. If you could see the whole plant, it would be wilted.

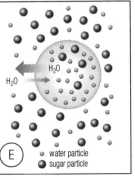

E
• water particle
● sugar particle

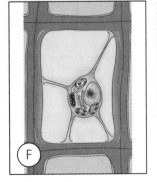

F

✔ *Reading Check*

2. If the concentration of water outside a cell is higher than it is inside a cell, in which direction will water move?

_____

_____

_____

Use with textbook pages 40–45.

Crossing the cell membrane

Vocabulary
diffusion
concentration
osmosis
a selectively permeable membrane

Use the terms in the vocabulary box to fill in the blanks. Each term may be used as often as necessary.

1. _____ refers to the amount of a substance in a given space.

2. _____ is the movement of particles from an area of higher concentration to an area of lower concentration.

3. _____ allows some materials to pass through it but keeps other materials out.

4. _____ is the diffusion of water molecules through a selectively permeable membrane.

5. _____ moves wastes from inside a cell to outside a cell.

6. _____ can be compared to a window screen.

7. _____ happens when water particles move from a place where their concentration is higher to a place where their concentration is lower.

8. _____ is the process by which oxygen is moved into a cell.

9. _____ is the process by which carbon dioxide is moved out of a cell.

Use with textbook pages 40–44.

Osmosis and diffusion

Compare and contrast diffusion and osmosis using this Venn diagram. On the left side list how diffusion is different from osmosis. On the right side list how osmosis is different from diffusion. In the middle section list how they are similar to each other.

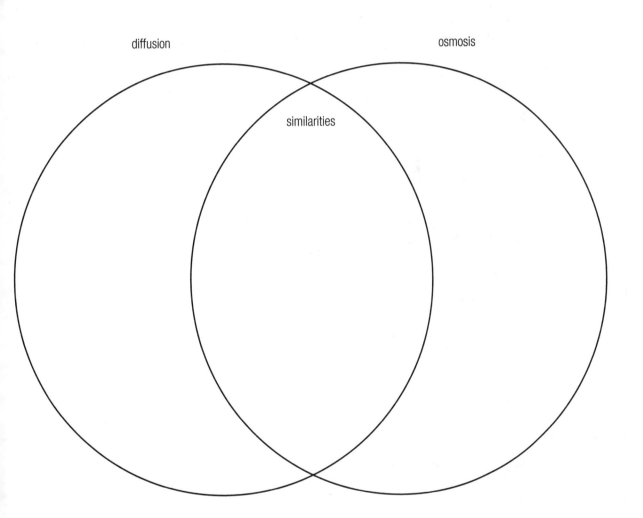

diffusion

osmosis

similarities

Use textbook pages 43–45.

Examples of osmosis

To predict the direction of water flow through a cell membrane, you have to compare the concentration of particles on both sides of the membrane. Examine the diagrams below. Explain why the plant cell looks different in each illustration.

Diagram	Explanation
A.	
B.	
C.	

Use with textbook pages 40–45.

Diffusion, osmosis, and the cell membrane

Circle the letter of the best answer.

1. Diffusion is

   A. the movement of particles from an area of low concentration to an area of high concentration

   B. the movement of particles to the inside of a cell only

   C. the movement of particles from an area of high concentration to an area of low concentration

   D. when the particles do not move through the cell membrane at all

2. Osmosis is

   A. the movement of water from an area of low concentration to an area of high concentration

   B. the movement of water to the inside of a cell only

   C. the movement of water from an area of high concentration to an area of low concentration

   D. when the water does not move through the cell membrane at all

3. A selectively permeable membrane

   A. keeps substances out of the cell

   B. keeps substances in the cell

   C. has many small openings

   D. allows only water to pass through it

Use the following diagram to answer questions 4 and 5.

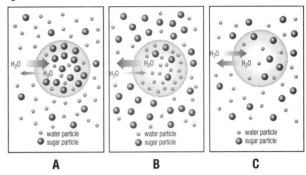

4. In which diagram(s) does water move into and out of the cell at the same rate?

   A. A

   B. B

   C. C

   D. both A and B

5. In which diagram(s) will the cell begin to swell?

   A. A

   B. B

   C. C

   D. both A and C

Match each Term on the left with the best Descriptor on the right. Each Descriptor may be used only once.	
Term	**Descriptor**
6. _____ concentration **7.** _____ diffusion **8.** _____ osmosis **9.** _____ selectively permeable membrane	**A.** moves oxygen into cells **B.** moves water into and out of cells **C.** allows some substances through **D.** surrounds the cell with water **E.** amount of a substance in a certain place

Body Systems

Textbook pages 52–63

Before You Read

In this section, you will find out about the systems of the human body. A system is made of two or more parts that work together as a whole. If one of the parts is missing or damaged, a system will not work well. It might not work at all. On the lines below, name one type of system in your home. Give an example of what might happen if one part of it is damaged.

_____

_____

 **Mark the Text**

Create an Outline
Make an outline of the information in this section. Use the headings in the reading as a starting point. Include the boldface terms and any other terms that you think are important.

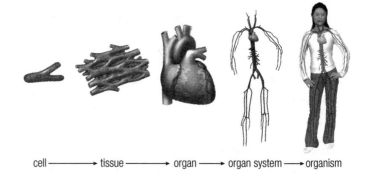

cell ⟶ tissue ⟶ organ ⟶ organ system ⟶ organism

What parts make up each system of the human body?

There are 11 systems of the body. Each of these systems is made up of different parts that work together as a whole to perform all the functions that keep you alive. The parts that make up each body system are cells, tissues, organs, and organ systems.

What is tissue?

Cells that have the same structure and that play the same role in the body are grouped together to form **tissue**. For instance, muscle cells are grouped to form muscle tissue. ✓

What is an organ?

Tissues of different kinds that work together form an **organ**. For instance, the heart is an organ. The heart is mostly made of muscle tissue. Nerve tissue transfers signals to the heart from the brain and from other parts of the body. Epithelial tissue lines the inside of the heart and covers the outside of it.

 **Reading Check**

1. What is a tissue?

_____

_____

_____

Connective tissue gives strength and shape to the other tissues that form the heart. Muscle tissue, nerve tissue, epithelial tissue, and connective tissue are also found in other organ systems. ✓

What is an organ system?

An organ can work by itself or it can work together with other organs to form an **organ system**. The heart is the only organ in the circulatory system. The digestive system has several different organs, including the stomach, the small intestine, and the large intestine. The organs of the digestive system work together to help you take in food, break it down, absorb nutrients, and remove solid wastes from your body.

✔ Reading Check

2. Which four tissues work together in the heart?

_____

_____

_____

Systems in the Human Body		
Circulatory – moves blood, nutrients, gases, and wastes	**Digestive** – takes in and breaks down food, absorbs nutrients, gets rid of solid waste	**Respiratory** – controls breathing and exchanging gases in lungs and tissues
Excretory – removes liquid and gas wastes	**Immune** – defends the body from infections	**Endocrine** – makes hormones
Reproductive – has organs for making babies	**Integumentary** (skin, hair, and nails) – protects the body	**Skeletal** – has bones that support the body and work with muscles to move the body
Muscular – has muscles that work with bones to move the body	**Nervous** – has nerves that detect, signal, and respond to changes in the environment	

Use with textbook pages 56–57.

Eleven body systems

Vocabulary	
circulatory	respiratory
immune	endocrine
reproductive	muscular
digestive	skeletal
defensive	excretory
integumentary	nervous

Use the terms in the vocabulary box to fill in the blanks. Use each term only once. You will not need to use every term.

1. The _____ system controls breathing.

2. The _____ system has bones that support the body and work with muscles to move the body.

3. The _____ system has nerves that detect, signal, and respond to changes in the environment.

4. The _____ system removes liquid and gas wastes from the body.

5. The _____ system makes hormones.

6. The _____ system takes in and breaks down food, absorbs nutrients, and gets rid of solid waste.

7. The _____ system protects the body and includes skin, hair, and nails.

8. The _____ system includes organs for making babies.

9. The _____ system defends the body against infections.

10. The _____ system has muscles that work with bones to move the body.

11. The _____ system moves blood, nutrients, gases, and wastes.

Use with textbook pages 54–62.

Body systems puzzle

Across	Down
2. a group of tissues working together to perform a task	1. system that includes hair, skin, and nails
3. a group of cells that have the same structure and function	4. system that exchanges gases in lungs and tissues
7. system that includes organs for making babies	5. system that includes nerves
	6. basic unit of life
	8. system that breaks down food

Use with textbook pages 56–57.

Name the system

Identify each of the following body systems.

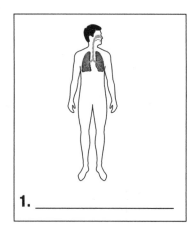

1. _____

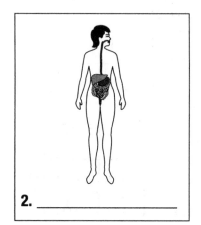

2. _____

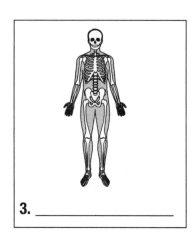

3. _____

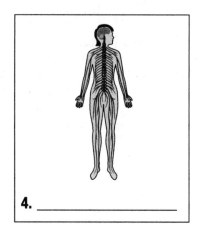

4. _____

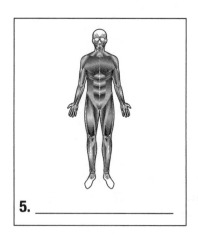

5. _____

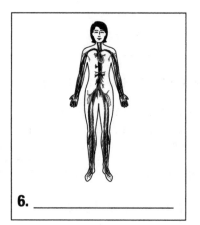

6. _____

Use with textbook pages 54–59.

Body systems

Match each Term on the left with the best Descriptor on the right. Each Descriptor may be used only once.

Term	Descriptor
1. _____ organ	A. a group of cells that have the same structure and function
2. _____ organ system	B. includes organs for making babies
3. _____ tissue	C. covers the outside of organs and the body
4. _____ muscle tissue	D. basic unit of all life
5. _____ nerve tissue	E. removes liquid from body
6. _____ connective tissue	F. transports blood, nutrients for survival
7. _____ epithelial tissue	G. a system that includes one or more organs
8. _____ integumentary system	H. gives strength and shape to the organs
9. _____ reproductive system	I. a group of tissues working together to perform a task
10. _____ endocrine system	J. includes skin, hair, and nails
11. _____ excretory system	K. transfers signals to the body and carries out a response
12. _____ circulatory system	L. helps to move body parts
	M. releases hormones

Circle the letter of the best answer.

13. This system has bones that support the body and work with muscles to move the body.

    A. respiratory

    B. muscular

    C. skeletal

    D. nervous

14. This system defends the body against infections.

    A. immune

    B. endocrine

    C. skeletal

    D. nervous

15. This system detects, signals, and responds to changes in the environment.

    A. endocrine

    B. muscular

    C. respiratory

    D. nervous

16. This system takes in and breaks down nutrients.

    A. immune

    B. reproductive

    C. digestive

    D. nervous

17. This system controls breathing.

    A. endocrine

    B. respiratory

    C. integumentary

    D. nervous

18. The organs in the digestive system include

    A. heart, stomach, lungs

    B. small intestine, large intestine, stomach

    C. only the heart

    D. none of the above

The Digestive and Excretory Systems

Textbook pages 64–81

Before You Read

Many structures and organs work together to digest food. What parts of your body do you think play a role? Write your thoughts on the lines below.

_____

_____

 *Mark the Text*

Create an Outline
Make an outline of this section. Use the headings in the reading as a starting point. Include the terms that you think are important.

 **Reading Check**

1. What are the five nutrients?

_____

_____

_____

_____

_____

What makes up the food you eat?

The food and liquids that you take into your body have nutrients. **Nutrients** are substances that supply the energy and materials your body needs. Your body uses nutrients to grow, develop, and repair itself. Water is not a nutrient but your body needs water to transport the nutrients and wastes.

There are five types of nutrients:

◆ Carbohydrates are the body's quickest source of energy. Examples: pasta and brown rice

◆ Proteins help to build muscles, skin, hair, and nails. Examples: fish and nuts

◆ Fats build cell membranes and are stored for energy. Examples: butter and oil

◆ Vitamins help keep your body healthy and strong. Examples: vitamin D from sunlight and vitamin C from oranges

◆ Minerals help keep your body healthy and strong. Examples: iron from leafy vegetables and calcium from milk ✓

How are nutrients from food digested?

The process of **digestion** breaks down nutrients, absorbs them, and stores some of them for later use. The digestive system also removes solid wastes that the body is not able to use. There are four stages of digestion. Read about them in the table on the next page.

The four stages of digestion	What parts of the digestive system are involved?	What happens?
1. ingesting	mouth	• Food is taken into the mouth.
2. digesting	mouth esophagus stomach small intestine	• Teeth grind food into smaller pieces. • Saliva mixes with the food pieces. • Muscles in the esophagus push the food down into the stomach. • The food is covered with **gastric juice**, which is a mixture of strong hydrochloric acid, mucus, and enzymes that break down the food into a liquid form. Enzymes are proteins that speed up digestion. The thick, slippery **mucus** protects the stomach lining from the strong acid. • The liquid food leaves the stomach and enters the first part of the small intestine, where it is broken down into small nutrient particles. Tubes connect to other organs, such as the pancreas, liver, and gall bladder, that produce substances to help digest the food.
3. absorbing	small intestine large intestine	• Nutrients are absorbed in the rest of the small intestine. • The small intestine is lined with many villi. **Villi** are fold-like structures that increase the surface available to absorb nutrients. • Undigested food leaves the small intestine and enters the large intestine, where water and some minerals are absorbed.
4. eliminating	rectum anus	• Any undigested material (feces) is stored in the rectum. • The feces leave the body through the anus.

Reading Check

2. What are the four stages of digestion?

_____

_____

_____

_____

How is liquid waste removed from the body?

Excretion is the job of the excretory system. **Excretion** removes liquid wastes and gas wastes from the body. Your kidneys filter liquid wastes from your blood and store the wastes (urine) in your bladder until they are flushed from the body.

Use with textbook pages 64–69.

Know your nutrients

Vocabulary	
brown rice	iron
butter	nuts
calcium	oil
circulatory	pasta
digestive	protein
energy	respiratory
excretory	villi
fish	vitamin C
gastric juice	vitamin D

Use the terms in the vocabulary box to fill in the blanks. Each term may be used more than once. You will not need to use every term.

1. Carbohydrates are the body's fastest source of _____

2. Examples of foods containing carbohydrates are _____
   and _____

3. _____ help build muscles, skin, hair, and nails.
   Examples of foods containing this nutrient are _____
   and _____.

4. Fats are used to build _____ and can be stored
   by the body for _____.

5. Examples of foods containing fats are _____
   and _____.

6. Two common minerals are _____
   and _____

7. Two common vitamins are _____
   and _____

8. The _____ system breaks down nutrients,
   absorbs them, and stores some of them for later use.

9. The _____ system removes liquid wastes and
   gas wastes from the body.

Use with textbook page 70.

Stages of digestion

Use a different colour for each stage of digestion. Colour in the areas of the digestive system where each of the stages occurs. Be sure to label each section.

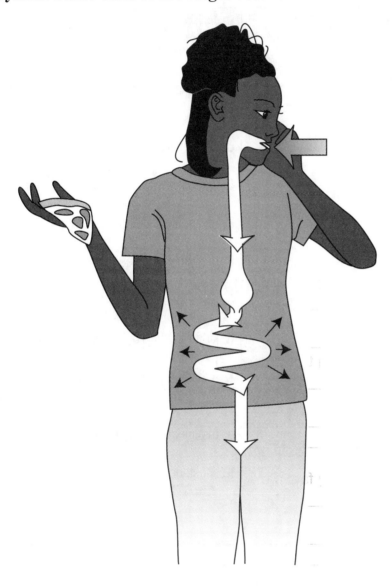

Use with textbook pages 71–76.

Looking inside digestion and excretion

**Match each Term on the left with the best Descriptor on the right.
Each Descriptor may be used only once. You will not need to use all the Descriptors.**

Term	Descriptor
1. _____ feces	**A.** a liquid in the stomach
2. _____ urine	**B.** fold-like structures that absorb nutrients in the small intestine
3. _____ villi	**C.** mixes with food pieces in the mouth
4. _____ gastric juice	**D.** undigested material leaves the body through this
5. _____ enzymes	**E.** undigested material stored in the rectum
6. _____ mucus	**F.** proteins that speed up digestion
7. _____ anus	**G.** liquid wastes stored in your bladder
8. _____ blood	**H.** kidneys filter liquid wastes from this
9. _____ saliva	**I.** a thick, slippery substance that protects the lining of the stomach
10. _____ nutrients	**J.** the liquid food that is broken down into nutrients
	K. substances that supply energy

se with textbook pages 64–80.

The digestive and excretory systems

Circle the letter of the best answer.

1. A nutrient used for quick energy is a

   A. protein

   B. carbohydrate

   C. fat

   D. mineral

2. A nutrient used to build cell membranes is a

   A. protein

   B. carbohydrate

   C. fat

   D. vitamin

3. A nutrient used to build muscle, skin, hair, and nails is a

   A. protein

   B. carbohydrate

   C. mineral

   D. vitamin

4. Iron and calcium are examples of

   A. minerals

   B. carbohydrates

   C. fats

   D. vitamins

5. The part of the digestive system in which undigested material is eliminated includes the

   A. rectum and anus

   B. pancreas, liver, and gall bladder

   C. large intestine

   D. none of the above

6. The part of the digestive system in which nutrients are absorbed includes the

   A. stomach and esophagus

   B. small intestine and large intestine

   C. stomach and small intestine

   D. all of the above

7. The part of the digestive system that ingests food is the

   A. mouth

   B. stomach

   C. esophagus

   D. all of the above

8. The part of the digestive system that digests food is the

   A. mouth and esophagus

   B. stomach

   C. small intestine

   D. all of the above

Match each Term on the left with the best Descriptor on the right. Each Descriptor may be used only once.	
Term	**Descriptor**
9. _____ digestion **10.** _____ excretion **11.** _____ gastric juice **12.** _____ mucus **13.** _____ nutrients **14.** _____ villi	**A.** thick slippery substance that protects the stomach lining **B.** breaks down, absorbs, and stores nutrients **C.** liquid in stomach **D.** fold-like structures that absorb nutrients **E.** mixes with food pieces in mouth **F.** substances that supply energy **G.** removes wastes

The Circulatory and Respiratory Systems

Textbook pages 82–95

Before You Read

How do you think oxygen from the air you breathe gets into your blood? Record your ideas below.

_____

_____

 Mark the Text

Check for Understanding
As you read this section, stop and reread any parts you do not understand. Highlight all the sentences that help you get a better understanding.

 **Reading Check**

1. Which blood vessels carry blood to the body from the heart?

_____

_____

_____

What structures and organs make up the circulatory system?

The **circulatory system** is the system that moves blood throughout the body. This system includes the heart, blood, and blood vessels.

The cells of your body need oxygen to work and stay healthy. **Blood** is a liquid mixture that includes red blood cells. Red blood cells carry the oxygen that body cells need. When body cells use oxygen, they make carbon dioxide gas as a waste. Red blood cells also carry this waste gas away so it can leave the body.

To reach all the cells of your body, blood moves through a network of tubes. These tubes are called blood vessels. There are three types of blood vessels.

♦ **Arteries** are thick-walled blood vessels that move blood rich with oxygen to all the cells of the body.

♦ **Veins** are thinner-walled blood vessels that bring blood back to the heart and lungs so it can be enriched with oxygen again.

♦ **Capillaries** are very thin blood vessels that link arteries with veins. Oxygen diffuses from capillaries into cells. Carbon dioxide diffuses from cells into capillaries. ✔

How does the heart work?

The role of the heart is to pump blood through the blood vessels.

The heart has four chambers. The two upper chambers are the right atrium and the left atrium. The two lower chambers are the right ventricle and the left ventricle. Blood moves through the heart in the order described on the next page.

Find each of these locations in the diagram below.

◆ Blood that is low in oxygen flows from veins into the right atrium.

◆ The right atrium sends this blood to the right ventricle.

◆ The right ventricle sends the blood to the lungs so that it can be enriched with oxygen.

◆ The oxygen-rich blood moves back from the lungs to the heart and enters the left atrium.

◆ The left atrium sends this blood to the left ventricle.

◆ The left ventricle sends oxygen-rich blood to the whole body through the arteries.

What structures and organs make up the respiratory system?

The **respiratory system** is made up of two lungs and a series of passages that bring oxygen into the body and move carbon dioxide out of it. The passages lead from the nose, down the throat, and into two air tubes called bronchi. These tubes branch into a series of smaller air tubes called bronchioles.

The bronchioles end at thin-walled sacs called **alveoli**. The alveoli are surrounded by many capillaries. During **gas exchange**, oxygen and carbon dioxide change places between the alveoli and the capillaries. Oxygen from the air you inhale moves from the alveoli into the blood in the capillaries. Now the blood is enriched with oxygen. It can go back to the heart to be pumped to the cells in the body. While the blood is enriched with oxygen, carbon dioxide waste moves from the blood in the capillaries to the alveoli. Now this waste gas can leave the body when you exhale. ✔

✔ **Reading Check**

2. Where does gas exchange take place?

_____

_____

_____

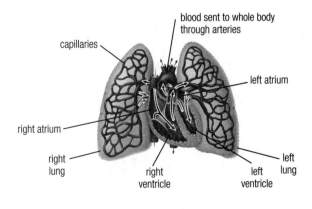

capillaries

blood sent to whole body through arteries

left atrium

right atrium

right lung

right ventricle

left ventricle

left lung

Use with textbook page 84.

Follow the blood through the heart

**Read the description below of how the blood travels through the heart. Number and
label each step in the diagram. The first step is numbered for you.
Then use a coloured pencil or pen to trace the flow of blood in the diagram from
number one all the way through to number six.**

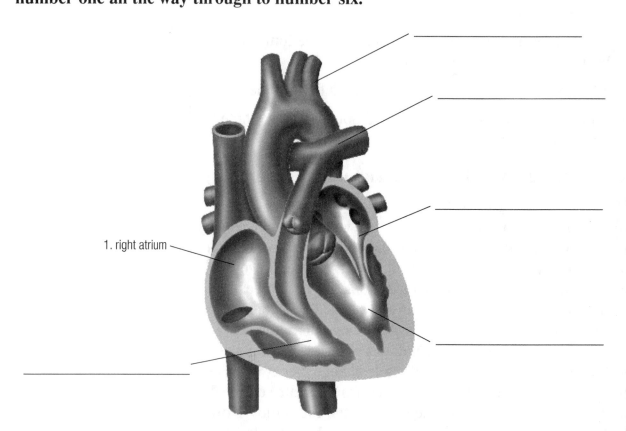

1. right atrium

1. Blood that is low in oxygen flows from veins into the right atrium.

2. The right atrium sends this blood to the right ventricle.

3. The right ventricle sends the blood to the two lungs so that it can be enriched with oxygen.

4. The oxygen-rich blood moves back from the lungs to the heart and enters the left atrium.

5. The left atrium sends this blood to the left ventricle.

6. The left ventricle sends oxygen-rich blood to the whole body through the arteries.

Use textbook pages 86–87.

Respiration match-up

Match each Term on the left with the best Descriptor on the right.	
Each Descriptor may be used only once. You will not need to use all the Descriptors.	

Term	Descriptor
1. _____ respiratory system	**A.** two air tubes
2. _____ alveoli	**B.** moves from the alveoli into the capillaries
3. _____ capillaries	**C.** made of two lungs and a series of passages
4. _____ bronchi	**D.** moves from the capillaries into the alveoli
5. _____ exhale	**E.** these surround the alveoli
6. _____ oxygen	**F.** oxygen and carbon dioxide do this in the respiratory system
7. _____ bronchioles	
8. _____ carbon dioxide	**G.** chamber in the heart
9. _____ inhale	**H.** oxygen enters your body when you do this
10. _____ change places	**I.** carbon dioxide leaves your body when you do this
	J. small tubes branching from bronchi
	K. thin-walled sacs

Use with textbook pages 86–87.

Blood vessels

Blood is carried from your heart through your body in three types of blood vessels.

Name each type of blood vessel and describe its job.

A.	B.	C.
Name: _____	Name: _____	Name: _____
Describe its job:	Describe its job:	Describe its job:

se with textbook pages 82–92.

The circulatory and respiratory systems

Circle the letter of the best answer.

1. Blood is transported to the heart through
   A. veins
   B. arteries
   C. capillaries
   D. bronchioles

2. Red blood cells
   A. carry the oxygen that body cells need
   B. carry away waste gas
   C. both A and B
   D. neither A nor B

3. The two upper chambers in the heart are
   A. the right ventricle and the left ventricle
   B. the right atrium and the left atrium
   C. the right ventricle and the right atrium
   D. the left ventricle and the left atrium

4. The heart is a(n)
   A. cell
   B. tissue
   C. organ
   D. organ system

5. Oxygen enters your body when you
   A. inhale
   B. exhale
   C. both A and B
   D. none of the above

6. Carbon dioxide leaves your body when you
   A. inhale
   B. exhale
   C. both A and B
   D. none of the above

7. The left ventricle sends oxygen-rich blood
   A. from the lungs to the heart
   B. to the two lungs
   C. from the veins into the right atrium
   D. to the whole body through the arteries

Match each Term on the left with the best Descriptor on the right. Each Descriptor may be used only once.

Term	Descriptor
8. _____ respiratory system	A. two air tubes
9. _____ circulatory system	B. bring blood back to the heart and lungs
10. _____ veins	C. thin-walled sacs
11. _____ arteries	D. this system moves blood throughout the body
12. _____ blood	E. move blood to all the cells in the body
13. _____ gas exchange	F. oxygen and carbon dioxide change places
14. _____ alveoli	G. mixture that includes red blood cells
15. _____ capillaries	H. this system brings oxygen into the body and moves carbon dioxide out of it
	I. link arteries with veins

The Immune System

Textbook pages 100–109

Before You Read

If you have a cold or the flu, you can spread the sickness to someone else. How does the sickness spread? Write your ideas on the lines below.

_____

_____

 **Mark the Text**

Create a Chart
Highlight the text that describes the body's two main lines of defence. In a different colour, highlight text that describes how the immune system attacks pathogens. Use the highlighted text to create a chart about how the immune system protects the body.

✔ Reading Check

1. What are the immune system's two lines of defence?

_____

_____

_____

What is the immune system?

Viruses and some kinds of bacteria can cause disease. Living things and substances that cause disease are called **pathogens**. They are found in the air, water, and soil—everywhere around you. Many of the diseases caused by pathogens are infectious. This means that the diseases can be passed on to other people through:

◆ direct contact, such as shaking hands or sharing drink containers

◆ indirect contact, such as sneezing without covering your mouth

◆ eating infected food or drinking infected water

◆ animal bites

How does the immune system protect the body?

The **immune system** is the body's defence system. It guards against pathogens and the diseases they cause.

The immune system's first line of defence is to keep pathogens out of the body. The skin stops many pathogens from entering the body. As well, the sweat and oils on your skin can kill pathogens. Gastric juice can destroy pathogens that enter the stomach. The mucus in your nose can help keep pathogens out of your respiratory system.

The immune system's second line of defence is to respond to pathogens by attacking them. There are two ways the immune system attacks pathogens. One way is an innate immune response. The other way is an acquired immune response. ✔

What is an innate immune response?

An innate immune response is a quick, general response that all living things are born with. When pathogens attack the human body, the body makes more white blood cells. **White blood cells** are cells that are carried in the blood to fight infections in the body. The white blood cells are sent to the part of the body that is infected by the pathogens. The white blood cells swallow up the invading pathogens.

What is an acquired immune response?

Normally, the immune system recognizes tissues and cells of the body as things that belong to the body. When the body is invaded by a foreign substance, the immune system recognizes it as *not* belonging. It can take up to a week to develop the response needed to defeat the invader.

   Any non-living substance that is foreign to the body and that triggers an immune response is called an **antigen**. A splinter, plant pollen, and a virus are all antigens.

How does the body start an acquired immune response against invaders?

One way that the body starts an acquired immune response involves white blood cells called B cells. B cells make substances called **antibodies**. Antibodies bind to antigens to make them harmless or mark them for destruction by other white blood cells.

   The other way that the body starts an acquired immune response involves white blood cells called helper T cells. Helper T cells find antigens and signal B cells to produce antibodies to attack them.

   When antigens are destroyed, some of the antibodies stay in the body. The antibodies provide active immunity. In other words, they can protect the body from future infections.

   Killer T cells are another type of white blood cell. These cells wipe out antigens and pathogens on their own.

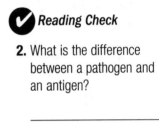

Reading Check

2. What is the difference between a pathogen and an antigen?

_____

_____

_____

Use with textbook pages 100–105.

Looking at the immune system

Vocabulary

acquired	immune
antibodies	infectious
antigens	innate
active immunity	pathogens
bacteria	second
first	white blood cells

Use the terms in the vocabulary box to fill in the blanks. You will not need to use every term.

1. Organisms, such as some bacteria, and substances, such as viruses, that cause disease are called _____.

2. _____ diseases can be passed to other people.

3. The _____ system is the body's defence system.

4. The immune system's _____ line of defence against infectious diseases includes the skin.

5. The immune system's _____ line of defence includes two types of immune response.

6. _____ are carried in the blood to fight infections in the body.

7. All living things are born with a(n) _____ immune response.

8. Non-living substances that are foreign to the body and trigger an immune response are called _____.

9. In the first process of an acquired immune response, B cells make substances called _____ that bind to antigens.

10. All acquired immune responses help give you _____.

Use with textbook page 101.

Infectious disease

**What are four ways diseases can be passed on to people? List the ways in the
blanks below. Then make a drawing to illustrate each way.**

1. _____

   _____

2. _____

   _____

3. _____

   _____

4. _____

   _____

Use with textbook pages 102–105.

Defence in action

The immune system's response to pathogens is a bit like the plot of an action movie. Describe or draw storyboards for an action movie about the immune system in the space below.

1.	2.	3.
4.	5.	6.

Use with textbook pages 100–109.

The immune system

Match each Term on the left with the best Descriptor on the right. Each Descriptor may be used only once.

Term	Descriptor
1. _____ first line of defence	**A.** sneezing without covering your mouth
2. _____ second line of defence	**B.** blood cells fight infection
3. _____ direct contact	**C.** a substance that triggers an immune response
4. _____ indirect contact	**D.** specific particles created by the immune system to destroy specific disease-causing invaders
5. _____ antigen	**E.** keeps pathogens out of the body
6. _____ pathogen	**F.** living things that cause disease
	G. shaking hands or sharing drink containers with an infected person

Circle the letter of the best answer.

7. Pathogens are kept out of your respiratory system by

  A. mucus

  B. sweat

  C. oils on your skin

  D. gastric juice

8. Pathogens on the skin can be killed by

  A. sweat

  B. oils on your skin

  C. A and B

  D. neither A nor B

9. The body's second line of defence is to

  A. attack pathogens

  B. recognize pathogens

  C. keep pathogens out of the body

  D. wait a week to develop a response to pathogens

10. Why are white blood cells sent to the part of the body that is infected by pathogens?

  A. to heal the infection

  B. to supply blood to the infected area

  C. to provide immunity

  D. to destroy the pathogens

11. What are the two types of immune response?

  A. first line and second line

  B. innate and acquired

  C. pathogen and antigen

  D. direct and indirect

12. What is the role of antibodies?

I.	bind to antigens to make them harmless
II.	mark antigens for later destruction
III.	protect the body from future infections
IV.	wipe out antigens on their own

  A. I, II, and III only

  B. II, III, and IV only

  C. I, III, and IV only

  D. I, II, III, and IV

13. The role of helper T cells is

  A. find antigens and signal B cells to produce antibodies

  B. wipe out antigens and pathogens on their own

  C. both A and B

  D. neither A nor B

Factors Affecting the Immune System

Textbook pages 110–117

Before You Read

You probably remember receiving a vaccination at school or in your doctor's office. How does a vaccination help you to stay healthy? Write your ideas on the lines below.

_____

_____

Mark the Text

In Your Own Words
Highlight the main idea in each paragraph. Stop after each paragraph and put what you just read into your own words.

Reading Check

1. Why are people given vaccines?

_____

_____

_____

How does a vaccine help the immune system?

A **vaccine** is a weakened or dead form of a disease pathogen. A vaccine may be given to a person by needle or by mouth.

Once a vaccine is in the body, the immune system starts to respond. The immune system makes antibodies against the antigens in the vaccine. This way, your body has antibodies to defend you if you are exposed to the live form of the pathogen.

Some vaccines are given early in life and once more when you are older. This additional vaccine helps to extend the immune system's memory for that antigen. Grade 9 students in British Columbia receive vaccines for at least three diseases: tetanus, diphtheria, and pertussis. You may also need vaccines later in life, especially if you travel to other parts of the world. ✔

How does an allergy affect the immune system?

If you have an **allergy**, your immune system is very sensitive to a substance, such as dust, mould, or some foods. Any substance that causes an allergic reaction is called an allergen.

The immune system releases a chemical called histamine to combat allergens when they enter the body. Histamine makes the nose run and the eyes water. People can take an antihistamine drug to help reduce the effects of histamine.

In severe cases, an allergic reaction to allergens such as bee-sting venom and peanuts can cause the throat to swell. A person can have great trouble breathing. People who have such extreme reactions keep medicine with them as a precaution.

How does AIDS affect the immune system?

AIDS is a disease that is caused by a type of virus called HIV. HIV stands for human immunodeficiency virus. HIV is a dangerous pathogen that attacks the helper T cells of the immune system. Without helper T cells, the body cannot trigger the action of killer T cells or B cells. As a result, a person can get very sick, and even die, from infections.

HIV can enter the body in semen or in blood. Infection from HIV can happen if a person has sex without a condom. Infection from HIV can also happen if a person shares a needle that has been in contact with infected blood. These unsafe practices are the main way that people acquire HIV.

There is no known cure for AIDS. Developing a vaccine for AIDS is very difficult because HIV keeps changing. New forms of HIV are discovered every year.

How can you take care of your immune system?

A healthy immune system helps to keep all your other body systems healthy. Here are some steps you can follow to take care of your immune system. ✔

Taking Care of Your Immune System
• Eat a well-balanced diet.
• Brush your teeth, shower or bathe, and wash your hands often.
• Keep your home clean.
• Avoid tobacco and other non-prescription drugs.
• Get plenty of rest and exercise.
• Keep your vaccinations up to date.
• Do not engage in activities that involve sharing bodily fluids with others.

✔ *Reading Check*

2. Why should you keep your immune system healthy?

_____

_____

_____

Use with textbook pages 112–114.

Disorders of the immune system

Vocabulary	
AIDS	dead
allergy	helper T cells
allergen	histamine
allergic reaction	HIV
antibodies	killer T cells
antigens	live
antihistamine	memory
B cells	vaccine
bodily fluids	

Use the terms in the vocabulary box to fill in the blanks. Use each term only once. You will not have to use every term.

1. A(n) _____ is a weakened or _____ form of a disease pathogen that is given to a person by needle or by mouth.

2. Once the vaccine is in the body, the immune system makes _____ against the _____ in the vaccine.

3. Antibodies made to fight the dead form of a pathogen will defend you if you are exposed to the _____ form of the pathogen.

4. Sometimes, you are given additional vaccines later in life to help extend the immune system's _____ for that antigen.

5. If your immune system is too sensitive you may have a(n) _____ to a substance, such as dust or mould.

6. In a(n)_____, the immune system releases a chemical called_____ to combat allergens.

7. A(n) _____ drug can help reduce the effects of histamine.

8. Any substance that causes an allergic reaction is called a(n) _____.

9. AIDS is caused by a dangerous pathogen called _____ which attacks the _____.

10. Without the helper T cells, the body cannot trigger the action of the _____ or the _____.

Use with textbook page 114.

True or false?

Read the statements about your immune system given below. If the statement is true, write "T" on the line in front of the statement. If it is false, write "F" and rewrite the statement to make it a true statement.

1. _____ If you have already been vaccinated, you do not need to be vaccinated again.

_____

_____

2. _____ HIV is transmitted only by semen.

_____

_____

3. _____ A vaccine is a live form of a disease pathogen.

_____

_____

4. _____ An antigen causes an allergic reaction.

_____

_____

5. _____ Histamine makes the nose run and the eyes water.

_____

_____

6. _____ AIDS is caused by a bacteria called HIV.

_____

_____

7. _____ There is no known cure for AIDS.

_____

_____

8. _____ HIV attacks the helper T cells.

_____

_____

Use with textbook page 114.

Show what you know

Choose one of the steps for taking care of your immune system. Create a poster in the space below to show other people why the step is important. Be sure to include both words and pictures.

se with textbook pages 110–117.

Factors affecting the immune system

Match each Term on the left with the best Descriptor on the right. Each Descriptor may be used only once.	
Term	**Descriptor**
1. _____ allergy **2.** _____ allergen **3.** _____ antibodies **4.** _____ histamine **5.** _____ vaccine	**A.** chemical produced by the body **B.** weakened form of pathogen **C.** fight against antigens **D.** high sensitivity to a substance **E.** reduces runny nose and watering eyes **F.** causes allergic reaction

Circle the letter of the best answer.

6. As of 2006, all Grade 9 students in British Columbia receive booster shots for

  A. tetanus, diphtheria, and pertussis

  B. tetanus, diphtheria, and smallpox

  C. tetanus, smallpox, and pertussis

  D. polio, smallpox, and diphtheria

7. A vaccine works by stimulating your immune system to

  A. produce more antigens

  B. reduce the number of T cells

  C. reduce the number of B cells

  D. produce more antibodies

8. HIV is not transmitted by

  A. blood

  B. semen

  C. dirty needles

  D. shaking hands

9. AIDS is caused by

  A. bacteria

  B. virus

  C. semen

  D. blood

10. How can you take care of your immune system?

I.	get plenty of rest and exercise
II.	avoid tobacco
III.	never share bodily fluids with other people
IV.	wash your hands often

  A. I, II, and III only

  B. II, III, and IV only

  C. I, III, and IV only

  D. I, II, III, and IV

11. In a severe allergic reaction

  A. a person may have great trouble breathing

  B. the immune system needs to make more antibodies

  C. a person could die from infection

  D. the immune system cannot trigger the B cells

12. HIV attacks

  A. the helper T cells

  B. the killer T cells

  C. the blood

  D. the semen

Properties of Waves

Textbook pages 134–143

Before You Read

In this section, you will find out about waves, such as water waves, sound waves, and radio waves. On the lines below, list devices you use that make or use waves.

Mark the Text

Identify Details

As you skim the section, use one colour to highlight the text that talks about parts of a wave. Use another colour to highlight other facts about waves.

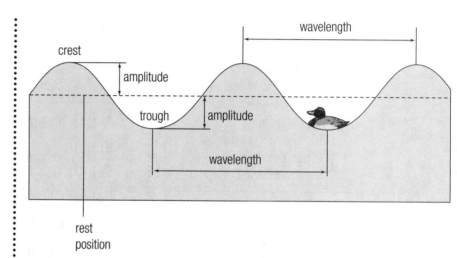

What are the features of a wave?

A **wave** is a movement that transfers energy through matter or space. Energy is the ability to apply a push or pull on an object. For example, a water wave moves energy through water. A sound wave moves energy through air. A radio wave can move energy through space.

Because you can see water waves, it is helpful to use a water wave to describe waves in general. You cannot see many other kinds of waves, such as sound waves.

A water wave does not carry water along with it. Only the energy carried by the water wave moves forward. A duck moves up and down as a wave passes — it does not move forward.

There are different features of waves that help you describe them. You can see these features labelled on the diagram above. The dotted line represents the rest position of the wave. This is also called the equilibrium position. For a water wave, the rest position of the wave is where the water would be if it were still.

Reading Check

1. What is the rest position of a water wave?

_____

_____

_____

The features of a wave are listed below.

◆ **crest:** the highest point of a wave

◆ **trough:** the lowest point of a wave

◆ **wavelength:** the distance from one point on a wave to the same point on the next wave, such as from crest to crest or from trough to trough. A wave with a long wavelength carries less energy than a wave with a short wavelength.

◆ **amplitude:** the height of a wave crest from its rest position. Amplitude is also the depth of a wave trough, as measured from its rest position. A wave with a large amplitude carries more energy than a wave with a small amplitude.

How many times does a wave repeat in a period of time?

Another important way to describe a wave is by its frequency. You may have already heard the term frequency used to describe radio stations or music. The **frequency** of a wave is the number of times it repeats in a given period of time. A repetition of a wave is also called an oscillation or vibration. One vibration occurs over one wavelength.

Frequency is measured in hertz. **Hertz (Hz)** means cycles per second.

When the wavelength is short, the frequency is high. When the wavelength is long, the frequency is low. ✓

What are the different types of waves?

You have read that sound travels by sound waves. Sound can travel through air, water, and even solid walls. The matter a wave travels through is called a **medium**. The medium can be a solid, liquid, or gas. For example, the medium of a water wave is water.

Not all waves need a medium. For example, visible light waves and radio waves can travel through space where there is no matter.

✔ *Reading Check*

2. How is the frequency of a wave measured?

_____

_____

_____

Use with textbook pages 134–136.

Features of a wave

Use the vocabulary words in the box below to label the parts of a wave.

Vocabulary	
amplitude	wavelength
crest	rest position
trough	

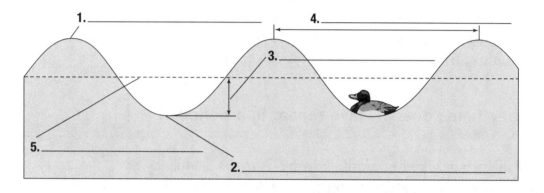

On the line beside each term, describe the wave feature.

6. amplitude _____

_____

7. crest _____

_____

8. trough _____

_____

9. wavelength _____

_____

10. rest position _____

_____

Name   Date

Use with textbook pages 134–138.

Characteristics of waves

Use the information in the graphs to answer the questions.

1. How long is the wavelength of the wave below? _____

2. How large is the amplitude of the wave below? _____

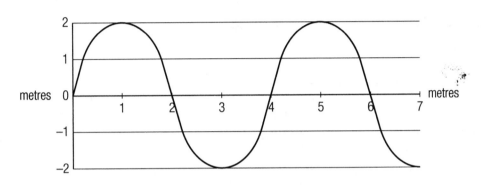

3. Which wave below has the smaller amplitude, A or B? _____

4. Which wave carries more energy, A or B? _____

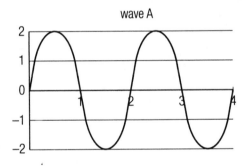

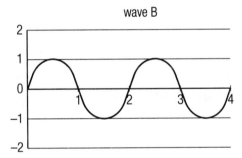

5. What is the same for waves X and Y below: amplitude, wavelength, or frequency?

_____

6. Which wave has a greater frequency, X or Y? _____

7. Which wave has a longer wavelength, X or Y? _____

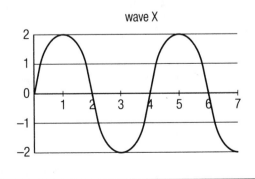

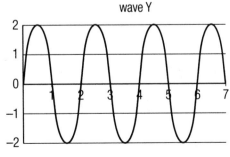

Use with textbook pages 134–138.

True or false?

Read the statements given below. If the statement is true, write "T" on the line in front of the sentence. If it is false, write "F," and then rewrite the statement so it is true.

1. _____ Waves transfer matter forward.

   _____

2. _____ Energy is the capacity to apply a push or pull to an object.

   _____

   _____

3. _____ A trough is the highest point in a wave.

   _____

4. _____ The wavelength is the distance from crest to trough.

   _____

5. _____ The amplitude of a wave is the height of a wave crest or the depth of a wave trough from the rest position.

   _____

   _____

6. _____ The larger the amplitude, the less energy is transported by the wave.

   _____

   _____

7. _____ Amplitude is the number of motions that occur in a given time.

   _____

   _____

8. _____ Frequency is measured in units called hertz.

   _____

9. _____ The wavelength of a wave increases as frequency increases.

   _____

   _____

se with textbook pages 134–138.

Properties of waves

Match each Term on the left with the best Descriptor on the right. Each Descriptor may be used only once.

Term	Descriptor
1. _____ crest 2. _____ trough 3. _____ amplitude 4. _____ frequency 5. _____ wavelength	A. height of crest from rest position B. a movement that carries energy through matter or space C. the lowest point of a wave D. trough to trough E. the highest point of a wave F. vibrations per second

Circle the letter of the best answer.

6. What happens when the amplitude of a wave becomes smaller?

  A. the frequency increases

  B. the wavelength decreases

  C. the height of the crests increases

  D. the amount of energy that the wave carries decreases

7. Which of the following is **not** a way to measure wavelength?

  A. the distance from crest to crest

  B. the distance from trough to trough

  C. the distance from the top of a crest to the bottom of a trough

  D. the distance covered by one complete crest plus one complete trough

8. Which of the following statements is true?

  A. The wavelength of a wave increases as the frequency increases.

  B. The wavelength of a wave increases as the frequency decreases.

  C. The wavelength of a wave decreases as the frequency decreases.

  D. The wavelength of a wave decreases as the frequency stays the same.

Use the following diagrams to answer questions 9 and 10.

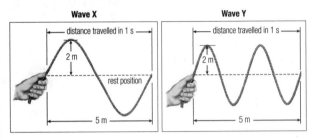

9. Wave X has a higher frequency than Wave Y.

  A. The statement is supported by the the diagrams.

  B. The statement is not supported by the diagrams.

  C. You cannot tell by looking at the diagrams.

10. Which statement is correct?

  A. Amplitude and wavelength are the same for both waves.

  B. Amplitude is the same for both waves.

  C. Wavelength is the same for both waves.

  D. Neither amplitude nor wavelength is the same for both waves.

Properties of Visible Light

Textbook pages 144–151

Before You Read

On the lines below, list five sources of light. One example is a light bulb.

_____

Create a Quiz

After you have read this section, create a quiz question for each paragraph. After you have written the quiz questions, be sure to answer them.

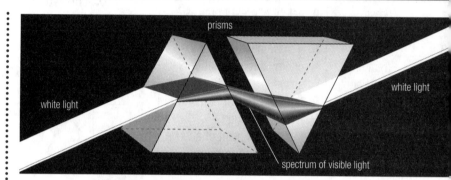

prisms

white light

white light

spectrum of visible light

What is visible light?

Scientists explain light using several models. One of these models is the **wave model of light**. In this model, **light** is a wave that travels through empty space. Like the waves that you learned about in section 4.1, light waves move energy from one place to another. **Visible light** is light that you can see. Visible light includes all the colours of the rainbow.

How do prisms affect light?

In the 17th century, English scientist Sir Isaac Newton found that white light, such as sunlight, is made up of light of different colours. The different colours are caused by light waves of different wavelengths.

How did Newton split the white light? He shone it through a prism. A prism is made of a clear solid, such as glass. You can see its shape in the diagram above. The light was split because a wave bends when it moves from one medium to another. This bending of a wave at the border between one medium and another is called **refraction**. When light enters a prism, the medium changes from air to glass. ✔

Light waves of different wavelengths refract at different angles. That is why the waves separate when they exit the prism. As the diagram shows, when you place a second prism near the first, you can cause the separated light to combine, forming white light again.

Reading Check

1. What is refraction?

_____

_____

_____

What are the colours of visible light?

Visible light is made up of a range of colours. People often put these colours into seven categories. The categories are: red, orange, yellow, green, blue, indigo, and violet. Different colours are light waves of different wavelengths. Red has the longest wavelength: around 700 nm (nanometres). Violet has the shortest wavelength: around 400 nm. The other colours have wavelengths between these two.

The seven colour categories of visible light are together known as the **visible spectrum**. The seven colour categories are sometimes abbreviated in the form of a person's name: ROY G BIV (**R**ed, **O**range, **Y**ellow, **G**reen, **B**lue, **I**ndigo, and **V**iolet).

Why do objects appear coloured?

Reflection occurs when a light wave strikes an object and bounces off. Different materials absorb and reflect different wavelengths of light. You see only the reflected wavelengths. A red ball looks red because it absorbs all wavelengths of visible light except for those around 700 nm. A black shirt looks black because it absorbs all the colours.

Objects appear black in the dark because they do not produce their own light. The colours you see come from other sources of light, such as the Sun or a light bulb. ✓

Reading Check

2. Why does a red ball look black in the dark?

_____

_____

_____

How do colours of light combine?

You only need three colours of light, such as red, green, and blue, to produce all the colours of the rainbow. These three colours are called the **additive primary colours** of light.

If you shine red, green, and blue light together, they produce white light. Adding two of these colours of light will produce a secondary colour of light as shown below.

primary colours of light		secondary colours of light
• blue light + green light	=	cyan light
• green light + red light	=	yellow light
• blue light + red light	=	magenta light

Use with textbook pages 144–149.

Colour your world

Look at the diagrams below. State the colour(s) of light indicated by "?".

1.

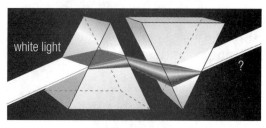

_____

2.

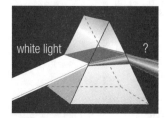

_____

3.

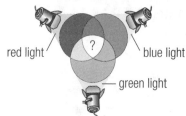

_____

4.

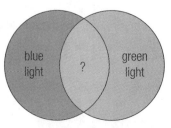

_____

5.

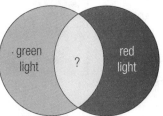

_____

6.

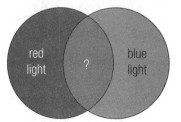

_____

se with textbook pages 144–149.

acts about visible light

Answer the questions below.

1. When white light is refracted through a prism, different colours emerge. Where do the different colours come from?

_____

_____

_____

2. Explain why all colours refract at different angles.

_____

_____

_____

3. When does light refract or bend?

_____

_____

4. Which colour in the visible spectrum has the longest wavelength?

_____

5. Which colour in the visible spectrum has the shortest wavelength?

_____

6. Explain how you can cause light separated by a prism to combine.

_____

_____

_____

7. Which has a higher frequency, yellow light or blue light?

_____

8. Why does a violet dress appear to be violet in sunlight?

_____

_____

9. List three colours that can combine to produce all the colours of the rainbow.

_____

Use with textbook pages 144–149.

Visible light

Vocabulary	
absorbed	refraction
amplitude	ROY G BIV
colour	spectrum
frequencies	visible light
prism	wave model of light
reflected	wavelengths
reflection	white light
refracted	

Use the terms in the vocabulary box to fill in the blanks. Use each term only once. You will not need to use every term.

1. The _____ describes light travelling as a wave.

2. _____ is light that you can see.

3. The bending or changing direction of a wave as it passes from one material to another is called _____.

4. White light is made up of waves having different _____ and _____.

5. Sir Isaac Newton demonstrated that _____ is a property of visible light.

6. A _____ refracts light into different colours.

7. When passed through a second prism, the _____ light is combined to form white light once again.

8. The seven colour categories of visible light are together known as the visible _____.

9. You can remember the order of the seven colours of the rainbow by using this abbreviation: _____.

10. A fire engine appears to be red because the colour red is _____.

11. A black shirt appears black because all colours are _____.

se *with textbook pages 144-149.*

Properties of visible light

Term	Descriptor
1. _____ light **2.** _____ spectrum **3.** _____ reflection **4.** _____ refraction **5.** _____ visible light **6.** _____ wave model of light	**A.** explains how light behaves like a wave **B.** light we can see **C.** a range of colours or frequencies of visible light **D.** occurs when a light wave is absorbed by an object **E.** occurs when a light wave bounces off an object **F.** bending of light wave as it passes from one material to another **G.** wave that travels through space

Match each Term on the left with the best Descriptor on the right. Each Descriptor may be used only once.

Circle the letter of the best answer.

7. Which of the following statements is true?

  A. White light has no colours in it.

  B. Sunlight emits only yellow light.

  C. There are six colours in the rainbow.

  D. You can see the colours of the rainbow when sunlight is refracted.

8. Which of the following statements is **incorrect**?

  A. Light travels like a wave.

  B. Colour is a property of visible light.

  C. A prism splits light into a spectrum.

  D. Each colour in the visible spectrum refracts at the same angle.

9. Which of the following correctly places the colours in order of shortest wavelength to longest wavelength?

	Shortest wavelength ⟶ Longest wavelength		
A.	red	green	violet
B.	violet	green	red
C.	green	red	violet
D.	violet	red	green

10. Which of the following colours has the lowest frequency?

  A. blue

  B. indigo

  C. orange

  D. yellow

11. Why does a blue car appear to be blue in the sunlight?

  A. The car reflects all the colours of the visible spectrum.

  B. The car absorbs the colour blue and reflects colours other than blue.

  C. The car refracts the colour blue and reflects colours other than blue.

  D. The car reflects the colour blue and absorbs colours other than blue.

12. Why does the print on this page appear to be black?

  A. The print reflects all the colours.

  B. The print absorbs all the colours.

  C. The print is made up of all the primary colours.

  D. The print is made up of all the secondary colours.

Light and the Electromagnetic Spectrum

Textbook pages 152–165

Before You Read

Choose a technology that uses invisible waves, such as microwave ovens, radio, X rays, or wireless Internet connections. Explain how the technology affects your life.

_____

_____

 **Mark the Text**

Identify Details
Highlight the names of different types of waves as you read them. Say their names aloud. Underline the names of technologies that depend on the waves.

What is the electromagnetic spectrum?

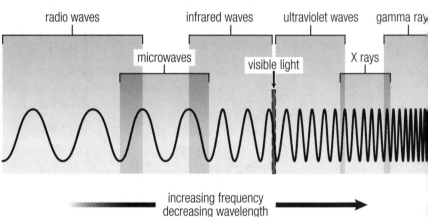

radio waves   infrared waves   ultraviolet waves   gamma ray

microwaves   visible light   X rays

increasing frequency
decreasing wavelength

Light that you can see is an example of a form of energy called **radiant energy**. This energy spreads out, or radiates, from its source in all directions. The Sun is a source of radiant energy. Radiant energy is not just visible light. The Sun and other sources of energy also give off energy in waves you cannot see. These waves transport energy by the vibration of electrical and magnetic fields. That is why these waves, including visible light waves, are known as **electromagnetic radiation**.

The spectrum of electromagnetic radiation is known as the **electromagnetic spectrum**. The electromagnetic spectrum includes radio waves, which can have wavelengths that are kilometres long. It also includes gamma rays, which can have wavelengths smaller than an atom. The spectrum includes all the electromagnetic waves in between. ✓

Reading Check

1. What larger spectrum of waves is the visible spectrum part of?

_____

_____

_____

What waves have wavelengths longer than visible light?

◆ **Radio waves** have the longest wavelengths in the electromagnetic spectrum. Radio waves are used for broadcasting radio and television signals. Radio waves are also used in medicine. They allow us to see inside our bodies using magnetic resonance imaging (MRI). **Microwaves** are a type of radio wave. As well as being used in microwave ovens, microwaves are also used to communicate with satellites.

◆ **Infrared waves** have wavelengths longer than red light in the visible spectrum. Heat lamps used by restaurants to keep food warm emit invisible infrared waves as well as red light. Infrared waves are also used in remote controls for televisions and for reading CD-ROMs. Infrared waves are also called heat radiation. ✔

What waves have wavelengths shorter than visible light?

◆ **Ultraviolet waves** have wavelengths shorter than violet light in the visible spectrum. Your body needs to absorb ultraviolet waves to make vitamin D. Too much exposure to ultraviolet waves, though, can result in sunburns and skin cancer. Ultraviolet waves are used to kill bacteria found in food, water, and on medical tools.

◆ **X rays** have shorter wavelengths and higher energy and frequencies than ultraviolet waves. X rays are used to photograph bones and teeth, to check the inside of baggage at airports, and to check jet engines and other machines for damage.

◆ **Gamma rays** have the shortest wavelengths, the highest energy, and the highest frequency of the electromagnetic spectrum. Gamma rays are used in radiation therapy to kill cancer cells.

✔ Reading Check

2. What are three uses for infrared waves?

_____

_____

_____

Use with textbook pages 152–160.

The electromagnetic spectrum

Write a use for each electromagnetic radiation stated below. In the box provided, draw a picture to illustrate your example.

1. Radio waves

Use: _____

2. Microwaves

Use: _____

3. Infrared waves

Use: _____

4. Ultraviolet rays

Use: _____

5. X rays

Use: _____

6. Gamma rays

Use: _____

se with textbook pages 152–160.

rue or false?

ead the statements given below. If the statement is true, write "T" on the line in ront of the statement. If it is false, write "F" and rewrite the statement to make it rue.

1. _____ Radiant energy spreads out from its source in all directions.

_____

_____

2. _____ Electromagnetic radiation includes only visible light waves.

_____

_____

3. _____ Microwaves are a type of infrared wave.

_____

_____

4. _____ X rays have more energy than gamma rays.

_____

_____

5. _____ Radio waves, microwaves, and ultraviolet waves all have longer wavelengths
          than visible light.

_____

_____

6. _____ Both X rays and gamma rays have higher frequencies than ultraviolet rays.

_____

_____

7. _____ Communicating with satellites is an application of gamma rays.

_____

_____

8. _____ The Sun radiates both visible energy and invisible energy.

_____

_____

Use with textbook pages 152–160.

More than meets the eye

Vocabulary	
electromagnetic radiation	radiant energy
electromagnetic spectrum	radio waves
frequency	ultraviolet rays
gamma rays	visible light
infrared waves	wavelength
microwaves	X rays

Use the terms in the vocabulary box to fill in the blanks. Use each term only once.

1. The _____ represents the different forms of electromagnetic radiation.

2. Light is classified as _____ because electrical and magnetic fields vibrate in a light wave.

3. _____ is energy that travels by radiation. An example of this is light.

4. Heat radiation, also known as _____, cannot be seen by your eyes but can be felt by your skin.

5. Microwaves are one type of _____ .

6. _____ can be used to communicate with satellites.

7. Because _____ have the highest energy of all electromagnetic radiation, they are the most damaging to human tissue.

8. Compared to all other types of electromagnetic radiation, radio waves have the lowest _____.

9. An overexposure to _____ can result in sunburns and skin cancer.

se *with textbook pages 152–160.*

Visible light and the electromagnetic spectrum

Match each Term on the left with the best Descriptor on the right. Each Descriptor may be used only once.

Term	Descriptor
1. _____ X rays	**A.** used to heat up left-over pizza
2. _____ microwaves	**B.** used to broadcast television
3. _____ gamma rays	**C.** used by computers to read CD-ROMS
4. _____ radio waves	**D.** used in radiation therapy to kill cancer cells
	E. used by dentists to take a picture of your teeth

Circle the letter of the best answer.

Use the following diagram of the electromagnetic spectrum to answer questions 5 to 10.

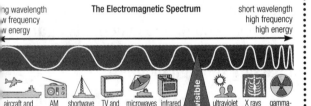

ng wavelength   The Electromagnetic Spectrum   short wavelength
w frequency   high frequency
w energy   high energy

aircraft and / hipping bands   AM radio   shortwave radio   TV and FM radio   microwaves Radar   infrared light   visible   ultraviolet light   X rays   gamma-rays

5. Which of the following types of radiation has the highest frequency?

A. visible light

B. infrared light

C. AM radio waves

D. gamma radiation

6. Which of the following is generally associated with radio waves?

A. visible radiation

B. high-energy waves

C. high-frequency waves

D. long-wavelength waves

7. Which of the following types of radiation gives off the lowest amount of energy?

A. X rays

B. visible light

C. microwaves

D. gamma rays

8. Which of the following correctly places these electromagnetic waves in order from shortest wavelength to longest wavelength?

A. visible light, radio waves, ultraviolet light, infrared radiation

B. radio waves, visible light, infrared radiation, ultraviolet light

C. ultraviolet light, visible light, infrared radiation, radio waves

D. ultraviolet light, infrared radiation, radio waves, visible light

9. Which of the following has a higher frequency than visible light?

A. infrared waves

B. X rays

C. microwaves

D. radio waves

10. How does the frequency of electromagnetic radiation change as wavelength of the radiation decreases?

A. it increases

B. it decreases

C. it stays the same

D. it increases and then decreases

The Ray Model of Light

Textbook pages 168–181

Before You Read

Light reflects from white paper and also from a mirror. Why can you see yourself in a mirror but not in the sheet of paper? Record your ideas on the lines below.

_____

_____

Create a Quiz
After you have read this section, create a five-question quiz based on what you have learned. Then answer your quiz questions.

✔ Reading Check
1. What three things can happen to light when it strikes a material?

_____

_____

_____

What can happen when light strikes different materials?

The ray model of light shows the direction of light as it moves in a straight line. You can use this model to show what happens when light strikes different materials. Three things can happen when light strikes a material.

1. The light may be transmitted (pass straight through it).

2. The light may be reflected (bounce off it).

3. The light may be absorbed (become "trapped" in it).

Each of these three outcomes affects what you see when light strikes a material. ✔

◆ If all or most of the light is transmitted, the material is **transparent**. Clear glass, air, and water are transparent because light passes through them.

◆ If all or most of the light is absorbed or reflected so that *none* of the light passes through, the material is **opaque**. A book, a metal can, and a wall are opaque because they block light from passing through them.

◆ If only some of the light is transmitted, and that light is scattered in all directions, the material is **translucent**. Waxed paper, clouds, and lampshades are translucent because they scatter the light that passes through them.

What happens when light reflects from a plane mirror?

When light reflects from a plane (flat) mirror, the rays of light bounce off the mirror in a regular pattern. The angle of an incoming light ray is the **angle of incidence** (*i*). The angle of the reflected ray is the **angle of reflection** (*r*).

he angle of incidence is always equal to the angle of
eflection. You can see yourself in a mirror because of this
egular reflecting pattern.

Even when light reflects from a rough, uneven surface, the
ngle of incidence of the light rays is still equal to the angle
f reflection of the light rays. However, on a rough surface,
ach light ray reflects at a different angle. In other words,
here is no regular pattern of reflection. That is why you
annot see yourself in a sheet of paper. ✔

ow is the angle of refraction different from the ngle of reflection?

.ight rays can refract, or bend. They refract when they move
rom one material into another, such as from water into air.
he **normal** is an imaginary line that passes through both
naterials at a right angle. If light rays slow down as they
efract, they bend toward the normal. If light rays speed up as
hey refract, they bend away from the normal. The **angle of
efraction** (*R*) is the angle of the ray of light that comes out
•f the boundary between the two materials, measured
»etween the refracted ray and the normal.

✔ Reading Check

2. How does the angle of
   incidence relate to the
   angle of reflection?

   _____

   _____

   _____

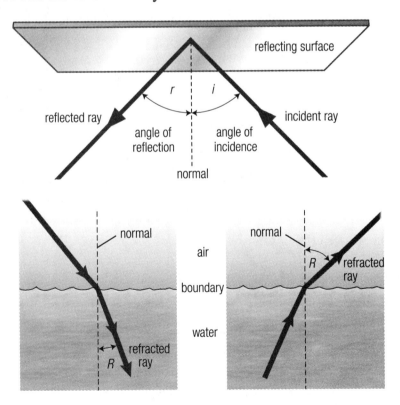

Use with textbook pages 169–170.

Getting in light's way

Complete the table and diagram below.

1. Complete the following table.

Materials	What happens when light strikes this material?	Examples of materials
transparent		1. _____ 2. _____
translucent		1. _____ 2. _____
opaque		1. _____ 2. _____

2. State whether light is mostly absorbed, reflected, transmitted, or scattered by each object.

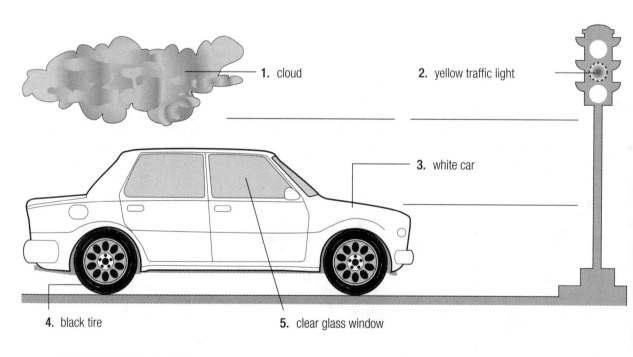

1. cloud

2. yellow traffic light

_____   _____

3. white car

_____

4. black tire

5. clear glass window

_____   _____

ame   Date

se with textbook pages 172–175.

Predictable behaviour of light

Complete the diagrams below.

1. Draw the light rays that result when light rays strike a transparent surface.

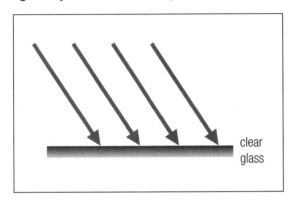

2. Draw the light rays that result when light rays strike a translucent surface.

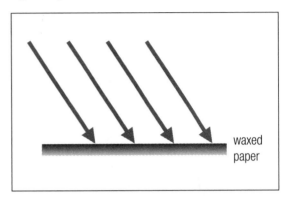

3. Draw the light rays that result when light rays strike an opaque surface.

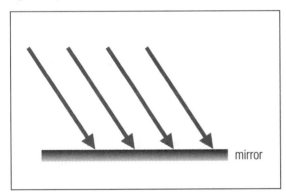

4. Label the angle of incidence and the angle of reflection.

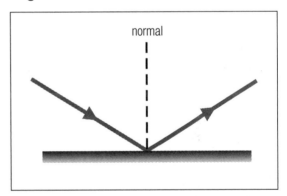

5. Draw the refracted ray that results when light passes from air to water. (Light travels more slowly in water than in air.)

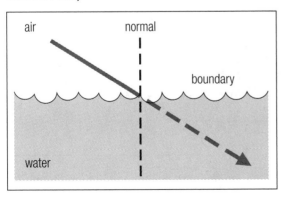

6. Draw the refracted ray that results when light passes from water to air. (Light travels more slowly in water than in air.)

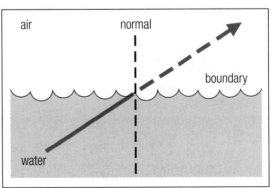

Use with textbook pages 168–175.

Light can reflect and refract

Vocabulary	
incidence	refracted ray
material	refraction
normal	sheet of paper
plane mirror	transparent
ray model of light	translucent
reflected ray	opaque
reflection	

Use the terms in the vocabulary box above to fill in the blanks. You will not need to use all the terms.

1. In the _____, light is described as a ray that travels in a straight path.

2. When light strikes _____ materials, it passes through them.

3. When light strikes _____ materials, it passes through them, but it is scattered from its straight path.

4. _____ materials do not allow light to pass through them.

5. The angle of reflection is equal to the angle of _____.

6. Light rays bounce off a _____ with a regular reflecting pattern.

7. The angle of _____ is the angle of a light ray that comes out of the boundary between two materials.

8. The angle of refraction is measured between the _____ and the normal.

se with textbook pages 168–181.

he ray model of light

Match each Term on the left with the best Descriptor on the right. Each Descriptor may be used only once.	
Term	**Descriptor**
1. _____ normal **2.** _____ angle of refraction **3.** _____ angle of reflection **4.** _____ angle of incidence	**A.** equal to the angle of reflection **B.** measured between the refracted ray and the normal **C.** angle of reflected ray **D.** imaginary line that passes through materials at right angle **E.** the surface that reflects

Circle the letter of the best answer.

5. Which of the following statements describes a property of light according to the ray model of light?

A. Light travels like waves.

B. Light travels in a straight line.

C. Light is made up of different colours.

D. Light has characteristics like frequency and wavelength.

6. If the angle of incidence is 50°, what is the angle of reflection?

A. 5°

B. 25°

C. 50°

D. 100°

Use the following diagram to answer questions 7 and 8.

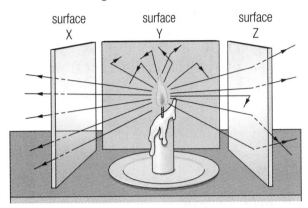

surface X surface Y surface Z

7. Which of the following is a translucent surface?

A. surface X

B. surface Y

C. surface Z

D. surface X and surface Z

8. Which of the following surfaces allow all the light rays to pass through?

A. surface X

B. surface Y

C. surface Z

D. surface X and surface Z

9. Which of the following correctly describes opaque objects?

I.	they can absorb all the light
II.	they can reflect all the light
III.	they do not allow light to pass through them
IV.	they transmit all light

A. I and III only

B. II and III only

C. III and IV only

D. I, II, and III

Using Mirrors to Form Images

Textbook pages 182–189

Before You Read

You stand in front of a mirror. In what ways is your reflection the same as you? In what ways is your reflection different from you? Write your ideas on the lines below.

_____

_____

Mark the Text

Identify Concepts
Highlight each question heading in this section. Then use a different colour to highlight the answers to the questions.

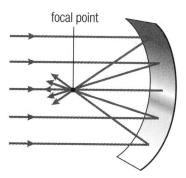

focal point

reflected light rays converge at the focal point

incoming light rays are parallel to one another

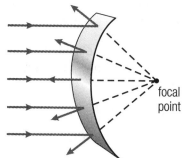

reflected light rays diverge so they do not meet

incoming light rays are parallel to one another

focal point

What are three common types of mirrors?

There are three common types of mirrors:

1. A plane mirror is a mirror with a flat surface. You might find a plane mirror on a bathroom wall or cabinet.

2. A **concave** mirror is a mirror that curves inward, like the inside of a spoon. A flashlight has a concave mirror behind the bulb. Shaving mirrors and make-up mirrors are concave, too.

3. A **convex** mirror is a mirror that curves outward, like the outside of a spoon. Some bicycle mirrors are convex. The large, curved mirrors that are used for security in many stores are convex, too. ✔

Reading Check

1. How is a concave mirror different from a convex mirror?

_____

_____

_____

© 2006 McGraw-Hill Ryerson Limited

What happens when light rays strike curved mirrors?

You learned what happens to light rays when they reflect from a plane mirror in section 5.1. Light rays behave in a different way when they reflect from curved mirrors.

The light rays that reflect from a concave mirror meet (converge) at a single point. This point is called a **focal point** because the light rays focus together there. Light rays that meet at a focal point are called **converging** light rays.

The light rays that reflect from a convex mirror spread out (diverge). Light rays that spread out after they reflect from a convex mirror are called **diverging** light rays. ✔

How do the images formed in mirrors compare?

All mirrors form images of objects because mirrors reflect the light that strikes them in a regular pattern. How the image looks depends on whether the mirror is flat or curved.

✔ *Reading Check*

2. What is the difference between light rays that are converging and light rays that are diverging?

_____

_____

_____

Appearance of image	Plane mirror	Concave mirror (if object is near the mirror)	Concave mirror (if object is far from the mirror)	Convex mirror
Object	Object as seen in plane mirror	Object as seen in concave mirror (near mirror)	Object as seen in concave mirror (farther from mirror)	Object as seen in convex mirror
Location	behind the mirror	behind the mirror	in front of the mirror	behind the mirror
Size	same size as object	larger than object	smaller than object	smaller than object
Shape	same shape	different shape	different shape	different shape
Left-right orientation	reversed	reversed	reversed	reversed
Up-and-down orientation	upright	upright	upside down	upright

Use with textbook pages 182–186.

Mirrors

Examine these diagrams. Then fill in the chart.

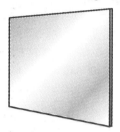

plane mirror

focal
point

convex mirror

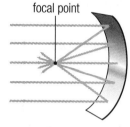
focal point

concave mirror

**On the first line, identify whether the mirror is plane, convex, or concave.
On the second and third lines, briefly explain how the mirror is used to see images.**

1. full-length bedroom mirror	**6.** jeweller's mirror
2. make-up mirror	**7.** car side-view mirror
3. car rear-view mirror	**8.** mirror in flashlight
4. dental mirror	**9.** shaving mirror
5. store security mirror	**10.** surface of a lake

Use with textbook pages 182–186.

Flat mirrors and curved mirrors

Complete the following table describing the three different types of mirrors.

	Plane Mirror	Concave Mirror (object near to mirror)	Concave Mirror (object far from mirror)	Convex Mirror
Is the reflecting surface of the mirror flat, curved inward, or curved outward?				
Is the image smaller, larger, or the same size as the object?				
Is the image upright or upside down?				
Is the image the same shape as the object?				
Does the image seem to be behind the mirror or in front of the mirror?				
Draw and label one example of how this type of mirror might be used.				

Use with textbook pages 182–186.

Mirror, mirror, on the wall

Vocabulary	
behind	images
concave mirror	in front
converging	plane mirror
convex mirror	reflect
diverging	upright
focal point	upside down

Use the terms in the vocabulary box to fill in the blanks. Use each term only once. You will not need to use every term.

1. All mirrors _____ light.

2. There are three types of mirrors. All three types reflect light rays to form

_____.

3. A _____ is a mirror that is flat and smooth. It produces an image that is the same as the object and appears to be the same distance from the mirror as the object.

4. A _____ is a mirror that curves inward. The image formed by this type of mirror depends on how far away the object is from the _____.

5. Light rays that come together at a focal point are described as

_____.

6. If the object is far from the concave mirror, its image is small and _____.

7. If the object is close to a concave mirror, then the image appears to be larger than the object and is _____.

8. A _____ is a mirror that curves outwards. It reflects parallel light rays as if they came from a focal point _____ the mirror.

9. Light rays that spread apart after reflecting are described as _____.

Use with textbook pages 182–189.

Using mirrors to form images

Match each Term on the left with the best Descriptor on the right. Each Descriptor may be used only once.

Term	Descriptor
1. _____ diverging	A. spreading apart
2. _____ converging	B. coming together
3. _____ plane mirror	C. curves inwards
	D. curves outwards
4. _____ convex mirror	E. is smooth and flat
	F. point where light rays meet
5. _____ concave mirror	

Circle the letter of the best answer.

6. Which of the following is used to make an image that is the same size as the object?

   A. plane mirror

   B. convex mirror

   C. concave mirror

   D. both concave and convex mirrors

7. What do all three types of mirrors have in common?

   A. they all produce upside down images

   B. they all reflect light rays to form an image

   C. they all reflect light rays so that the rays diverge and do not meet

   D. they all reflect light rays so that the rays converge on a focal point

8. What type of image would you expect to see if you looked at yourself in the bowl of a spoon?

   A. an upright, larger image of yourself

   B. an upright, smaller image of yourself

   C. an upside down, larger image of yourself

   D. an upside down, smaller image of yourself

9. Which of the following mirrors can produce an upright image?

I.	plane mirror
II.	convex mirror
III.	concave mirror

   A. I and II only

   B. I and III only

   C. II and III only

   D. I, II, and III

10. Which of the following mirrors can be used to make you look taller?

   A. plane mirror

   B. convex mirror

   C. concave mirror

   D. both convex and concave mirrors

11. Which of the following statements is **incorrect** about a plane mirror?

   A. It reverses left and right.

   B. It produces an image in front of the mirror.

   C. It produces an image that is the same size as the object.

   D. It produces an image that appears to be the same distance from the mirror as the object.

Using Lenses to Form Images

Textbook pages 190–199

Before You Read

Many common devices, such as eyeglasses and magnifying glasses, have lenses. What are lenses used for? Record your ideas in the lines below.

_____

_____

State the Main Ideas

As you read this section, stop after each paragraph. Put what you have just read into your own words.

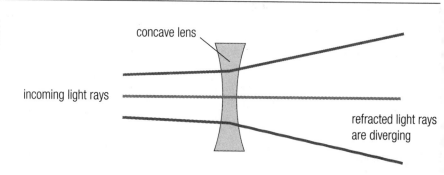

concave lens

incoming light rays

refracted light rays are diverging

What is a lens?

A **lens** is a piece of transparent material that is curved so that light rays will refract as they pass through it. The more curved the sides of a lens are, the more a ray of light will refract as it passes through the lens. There are two types of lenses: concave and convex.

What is a concave lens?

A **concave lens**

◆ is thinner in the middle and thicker at the edges

◆ refracts light rays that pass through it away from the normal. The light rays diverge and do not meet at a focal point.

◆ forms images that are upright

◆ forms images that are smaller than the object

 **Reading Check**

1. What happens to light rays that pass through a concave lens?

_____

_____

_____

What is a convex lens?

A **convex lens**

◆ is thicker in the middle and thinner at the edges.
◆ refracts light rays that pass through it toward the normal. The light rays converge at a focal point.

The image formed by a convex lens depends on how far the object is from the focal point. The distance from the centre of the lens to the focal point is called the **focal length**.

◆ If an object is between the lens and the focal point (less than one focal length), the image is upright and larger than the object.

◆ If an object is more than one focal length away from the lens, the image is upside down and smaller than the object ✓

Distance of an object from the convex lens	How the image compares with the object
more than two focal lengths	upside down and smaller
between one and two focal lengths	upside down and larger
directly at the focal point	no image forms
less than one focal length	upright and larger

Reading Check

2. What is the focal length of a lens?

_____

_____

_____

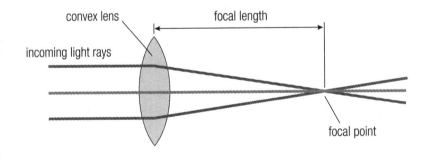

convex lens
focal length
incoming light rays
focal point

Use with textbook pages 190–193.

Light rays and lenses

1. Will the image be

   (a) larger, smaller, or the same size as the object?

   _____

   (b) upright or upside down?

   _____

more than 2 focal lengths

---

2. Will the image be

   (a) larger, smaller, or the same size as the object?

   _____

   (b) upright or upside down?

   _____

between 1 and 2 focal lengths

---

3. Will the image be

   (a) larger, smaller, or the same size as the object?

   _____

   (b) upright or upside down?

   _____

between 1 and 2 focal lengths

---

4. Will the image be

   (a) larger, smaller, or the same size as the object?

   _____

   (b) upright or upside down?

   _____

more than 2 focal lengths

Use with textbook pages 190–193.

Concave lenses and convex lenses

Compare and contrast concave lenses and convex lenses.

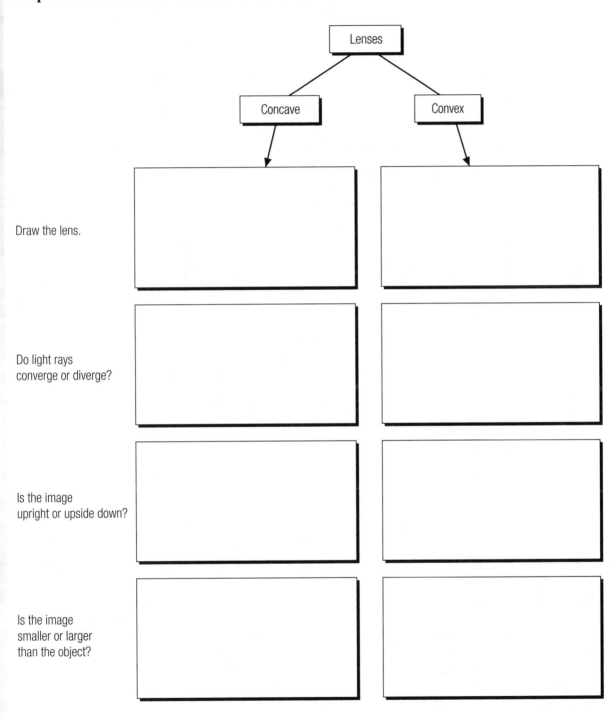

	Concave	Convex
Draw the lens.		
Do light rays converge or diverge?		
Is the image upright or upside down?		
Is the image smaller or larger than the object?		

Use with textbook pages 167–193.

Lenses puzzle

Use the clues to help you solve the crossword puzzle.

Across

3. a concave lens refracts light rays _____ the normal
5. mirror that curves outwards
6. if the object is more than two focal lengths from a convex lens, it will appear to be _____
9. the focal _____ is the distance from the centre of the lens to where light rays converge
13. light rays coming together
14. a concave lens is _____ in the middle

Down

1. if the object is less than one focal length from a convex lens, it will appear to be upright and _____
2. light rays meet at the focal _____
4. if the object is one or more focal lengths from a convex lens, it will appear to be _____
7. a convex lens refracts light rays _____ the normal
8. images formed by concave lenses are always smaller and _____
10. a concave lens is _____ at the edges
11. light rays spreading apart
12. mirror that curves inward

Use with textbook pages 190–193.

Using lenses to form images

Term	Descriptor
Match the Term on the left with the best Descriptor on the right. Each Descriptor may be used only once.	
1. _____ lens	**A.** point where the converging light rays meet
2. _____ focal length	**B.** a piece of transparent material that bends light
3. _____ convex lens	**C.** lens that is thinner in the middle than at the edge
4. _____ concave lens	**D.** lens that is thicker in the middle than at the edge
	E. distance from the centre of the lens to the focal point

Circle the letter of the best answer.

5. What happens to the light rays that pass through a convex lens?

A. all the light rays diverge

B. all the light rays converge

C. all the light rays are absorbed by the lens

D. some light rays diverge and some light rays converge

6. Describe the image that is produced by a concave lens.

A. it is upright and larger than the object

B. it is upright and smaller than the object

C. it is upside down and larger than the object

D. it is upside down and smaller than the object

7. Which of the following is a concave lens?

A. **C.**

B. **D.**

8. A concave lens reflects light rays

A. towards the normal

B. away from the normal

C. along the normal

D. none of the above

9. A convex lens reflects light rays

A. towards the normal

B. away from the normal

C. along the normal

D. none of the above

10. Light rays converge

A. at the focal length

B. at the focal point

C. inside the lens

D. on the edge of the lens

11. If the object is more than two focal lengths from a convex lens, the image will be

A. upside down and smaller

B. upside down and larger

C. upright and larger

D. no image forms

Human Vision

Textbook pages 202–215

Before You Read

Some people can see things clearly from a great distance. Other people can see things clearly only when they are nearby. Why might this be? Write your thoughts below.

_____

_____

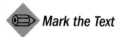 **Mark the Text**

Identify Details
As you read the section, use one colour to highlight the text or labels that describe the parts of the eye. Use another colour to highlight facts about light and human vision.

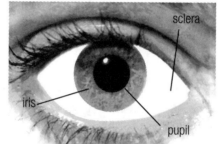

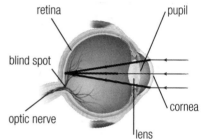

The image of an object that is formed on the retina is upside down. Follow the light rays below to see why.

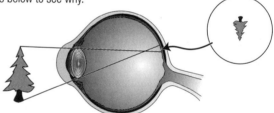

✔ **Reading Check**

1. What is the path of light rays from outside the eye to the retina?

_____

_____

_____

What happens to light that enters the eye?

1. First, light rays are refracted by the cornea. The cornea does most of the focussing of the light rays.

2. Next, the refracted rays enter the eye through the pupil. The iris changes the size of the pupil. The pupil gets larger to let more light in if light levels are dim. The pupil gets smaller to let less light in if light levels are bright.

3. Then the light rays pass through the lens. They converge on the retina. The lens gets thicker to help focus light rays from objects that are closer to you. The lens gets thinner to help focus light rays from objects that are farther away.

4. The image formed on the retina is upside down. Cells in the retina change the image into electrical signals.

5. The electrical signals are sent to the brain along the optic nerve. As the brain interprets the signals, it changes the image so that it is upright. ✔

Name

Date

Section

6.1

Summary

continued

How can lenses help correct vision problems?

◆ Near-sightedness: A person who is near-sighted can see objects clearly when they are close to the eye. Distant objects look fuzzy. This condition happens if the light rays converge before they reach the retina. A concave lens can help diverge the light rays before they reach the cornea. Then, as the light rays pass into the eye, they will converge on the retina to form a clear image.

◆ Far-sightedness: A person who is far-sighted can see objects clearly when they are far from the eye. Nearby objects look fuzzy. This condition happens if the light rays do not converge by the time they reach the retina. A convex lens can help the light rays to start to converge before they reach the cornea. Then, as the light rays pass into the eye, they converge on the retina to form a clear image.

◆ Astigmatism: If the shape of the cornea is irregular, light rays can focus in more than one place on the retina, resulting in a condition called **astigmatism**. This problem can also be corrected using lenses. ◉

✓ *Reading Check*

2. What are three reasons why an image might look fuzzy?

_____

_____

_____

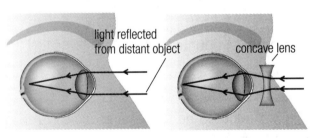

Near-sighted vision: image falls short of retina (eye has longer shape than normal eye)

Vision corrected with concave lens: lens allows image to fall on retina

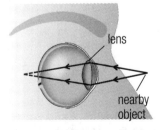

Far-sighted vision: image falls behind retina (eye has shorter shape than normal eye)

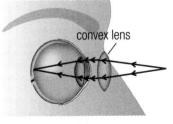

Vision corrected with convex lens: lens allows image to fall on retina

Use with textbook pages 202–210.

Parts of the eye

Use the vocabulary words in the box below to label the parts of the eye. Place the correct letter on the line next to each part of the eye.

Vocabulary

a. iris
b. lens
c. pupil
d. sclera
e. retina
f. cornea
g. optic nerve

1. _____ 2. _____ 4. _____

3. _____ 5. _____ 6. _____ 7. _____

Use the same vocabulary words in the box above to fill in the blanks below. Each word can be used only once.

8. Light rays are first refracted by the _____.

9. Surrounding the cornea is an opaque white tissue called the _____.

10. Light enters the eye through an opening in the centre called the

_____.

11. The _____ is the coloured circle of muscle surrounding the pupil. It controls the amount of light entering the eye.

12. Light then passes through the flexible, convex _____ which can change its shape.

13. Once light is refracted by the lens, it is focussed on the _____ at the back of the eye, where an image is formed.

14. Light-sensitive cells detect the image and an electric message is sent to the brain through the _____.

Use with textbook pages 202–210.

Inside the eye

Part of each statement below is false. Rewrite each statement to make it true.

1. The lens does most of the focussing of the light rays that pass through the eye.

_____

_____

_____

2. The light rays that pass through the eye diverge.

_____

_____

3. In bright light, the iris makes the pupil larger to allow more light to enter.

_____

_____

_____

4. The human eye has a concave lens.

_____

_____

5. The lens of the eye produces an upright image.

_____

_____

6. Light rays are sent to the brain through the optic nerve.

_____

_____

7. People who are near-sighted cannot bring nearby objects into focus.

_____

_____

8. Far-sightedness can be corrected by using a concave lens.

_____

_____

Use with textbook pages 208–209.

Vision problems

Complete the following table. One answer is provided for you.

Problem	Description	Where is image formed?	How is the problem corrected?
Near-sightedness	Nearby objects are clear, but distant objects are fuzzy.		
Far-sightedness			
Astigmatism			

Use with textbook pages 202–210.

Human vision

Match each Term on the left with the best Descriptor on the right. Each Descriptor may only be used once.

Term	Descriptor
1. _____ normal vision	**A.** image forms behind the retina
2. _____ astigmatism	**B.** image forms in front of the retina
3. _____ far-sightedness	**C.** no image is formed
4. _____ near-sightedness	**D.** image forms on more than one point on the retina
	E. image forms on the retina

Circle the letter of the best answer.

5. Which of the following is referred to when we speak about the colour of someone's eyes?

   A. iris

   B. pupil

   C. retina

   D. sclera

6. Which of the following is the white part of the eye?

   A. iris

   B. pupil

   C. sclera

   D. cornea

7. Which of the following statements is **true**?

   A. The pupil is larger in dim light.

   B. The pupil never changes in size.

   C. The pupil is smaller in dim light.

   D. The pupil is larger in bright light.

Use the following diagram to answer questions 8 to 10.

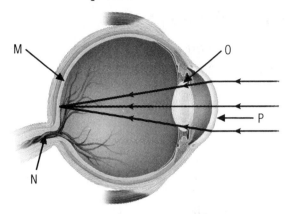

8. Which of the following structures represents the convex lens of the eye?

   A. M

   B. N

   C. O

   D. P

9. What is the function of the structure labelled N in the diagram?

   A. to focus the light

   B. to send electrical signals to the brain

   C. to provide nutrients and support for the cornea

   D. to control the amount of light that enters the eye

10. Which structure does most of the focussing?

   A. M

   B. N

   C. O

   D. P

11. Which of the following describes how the image of an object appears on the retina?

   A. it is reversed right to left

   B. it is upright

   C. it is upside down

   D. it is a mirror image of the actual object

Extending Human Vision

Textbook pages 216–229

Before You Read

How could you use lenses and mirrors to help you see an object that is very tiny or far away? Write your ideas on the lines below.

_____

_____

Create a Quiz

After you have read this section, create a quiz with five questions based on what you have learned. Trade your quiz with a partner. Answer each other's questions.

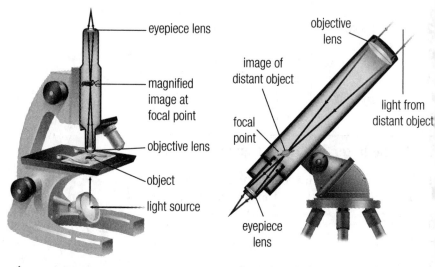

microscope   refracting telescope

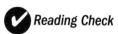 **Reading Check**

1. What kind of lens is used in a microscope and a refracting telescope?

_____

_____

How does a microscope work?

A microscope magnifies small, close objects so that they look larger than their real size. In a compound light microscope, a convex lens makes an enlarged image inside the microscope tube. The light rays from that image then pass through another convex lens in the eyepiece. This magnifies the image even more.

How does a telescope work?

A telescope magnifies distant objects. In a **refracting telescope** a convex lens gathers light from the object and focusses it into an enlarged image. The light rays from that image then pass through a convex eyepiece lens to magnify the image even more. Binoculars are actually two refracting telescopes placed side by side. ✓

In a **reflecting telescope** a concave mirror gathers the
ght from a distant object. A plane mirror reflects the light
athered by the concave mirror toward the side of the
lescope tube. The image that forms there is magnified by a
onvex eyepiece lens.

ow can you record what you see?

camera works in much the same way as the eye to form an
nage. A camera has an opening to let light in, just as the eye
as a pupil. In each case, the size of the opening can be
ontrolled to let in more or less light.

The camera and the eye each have a convex lens to gather
nd focus light into an image. A camera has a light detector
at acts like the retina of the eye. The light detector changes
ght into electric signals. The electrical signals are changed
to a picture. The picture can be stored or printed.

ow do you bring an object into focus?

devices like cameras, telescopes, and microscopes, you can
ake a clear image by focussing. Focussing means changing
e distance between the objective lens and the eyepiece lens
· screen so that the light rays converge on the screen.

ow does laser light extend human vision?

aser light** is light that has just one wavelength. Laser light
an carry a large amount of energy. This makes it useful as a
ol for surgery, such as eye surgery.

Laser light is also used in optical fibre technology. An
tical fibre is a very thin transparent tube that can transmit
ser light from one place to another, even around corners.
he laser light enters one end of the fibre and keeps
flecting off the smooth inside walls until it reaches the other
ad. This type of reflection is called **total internal reflection**.

The light in optical fibres can be used to carry sound,
ovie, and Internet signals. A tiny camera on one end of an
otical fibre can send pictures to a monitor and let surgeons
ew the inside of the body. ✅

✔ *Reading Check*

2. What are two ways that
laser light is used?

_____

_____

_____

Use with textbook pages 216–225.

Using optical systems

Vocabulary	
binoculars	magnifies
concave	microscope
converge	optical fibres
convex	plane
diverge	reflecting
eyepiece	refracting
laser light	total internal reflection

Use the terms in the vocabulary box to fill in the blanks. Use each term only once. You do not need to use all the terms.

1. A compound light _____ uses two

_____ lenses.

2. A microscope _____ small objects by forming

an enlarged image of the object.

3. A _____ telescope has a convex lens to collect

refract, and focus light rays from distant objects and a convex eyepiece to magnify

the image.

4. A _____ telescope uses a concave mirror, a

_____ mirror, and a convex lens to collect and

focus light from distant objects.

5. _____ are actually two refracting telescopes pu

side by side.

6. All the light in _____ has the same wavelength

and moves in the same direction.

7. Almost no light is lost or absorbed in _____,

which are transparent glass fibres.

8. _____ occurs when a light ray strikes the wall o

the fibre and is reflected back into it.

se with textbook page 219.

Compare a telescope and a microscope

Vocabulary	
concave mirror	light from distant object
eyepiece lens	light from light source
focal point	objective lens

Use the vocabulary words above to label the parts below.

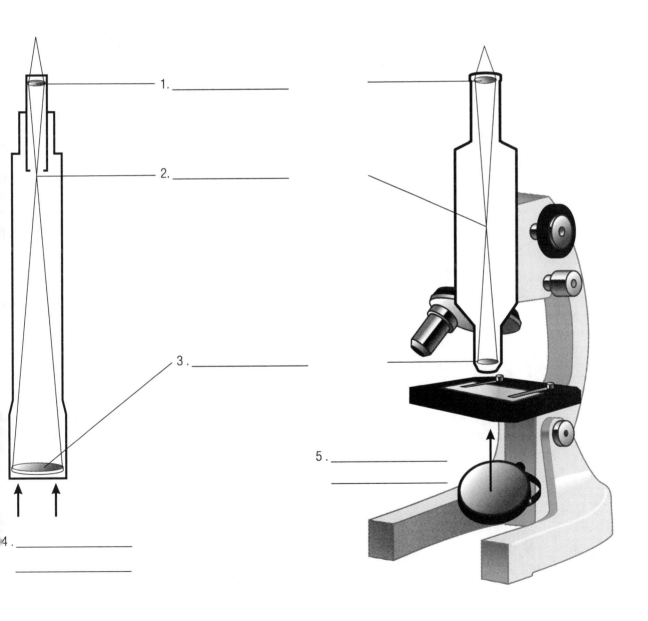

1. _____

2. _____

3. _____

5. _____

_____

4. _____

_____

telescope   microscope

Use with textbook pages 216–225.

Now you see it!

What kind of optical device could you design to help improve sight? Invent a device that uses lenses and mirrors. You might want to use laser light or optical fibres as well. Be creative! Draw your design below and explain what it does. Add labels to identify the parts.

se with textbook pages 216–225.

Extending human vision

Match each Term on the left with the best Descriptor on the right. Each Descriptor may be used only once.

Term	Descriptor
1. _____ camera 2. _____ binoculars 3. _____ microscope 4. _____ reflecting telescope 5. _____ refracting telescope	A. uses two lenses to see the Moon B. used to magnify small, close objects C. used to transmit telephone and Internet signals D. uses a concave mirror, a plane mirror, and a convex lens to see distant stars E. design is similar to the eye; uses a convex lens F. made of two refracting telescopes

Circle the letter of the best answer.

6. What does the term "focus" mean?

  A. to make the image look larger than the real size

  B. to absorb light and record a tiny part of the whole image

  C. to make light strike a boundary between two materials causing it to reflect

  D. to make a clear image by adjusting the distance between the screen and the lens

7. During which situation does an image appear focussed?

  A. when light rays diverge on the screen

  B. when light rays converge on the screen

  C. when light rays converge behind the screen

  D. when light rays converge in front of the screen

8. What does a microscope use to magnify objects?

  A. one convex lens

  B. two convex lenses

  C. two concave lenses

  D. a convex lens and a concave lens

9. Which of the following applies to both refracting telescopes and microscopes?

I.	uses only two lenses
II.	gathers and focusses light into an enlarged image
III.	light rays pass through a convex eyepiece lens to magnify objects even more

  A. I and II only

  B. I and III only

  C. II and III only

  D. I, II, and III

10. Which of the following is **false** about optical fibres?

  A. can transmit laser light

  B. are opaque glass fibres

  C. make use of total internal reflection

  D. used in telecommunications and in medicine

11. Which of the following is **false** about laser light?

  A. is used in surgery

  B. is just one wavelength

  C. carries a small amount of energy

  D. has all the crests and troughs lined up

States of Matter

Textbook pages 246–253

Before You Read

Water can be found in three forms called states. One state is liquid. Ice is what we call water when it is a solid. Water vapour is what we call water when it is a gas. How are these three states of water alike and different? Write your thoughts below.

Mark the Text

Identify Concepts
Highlight each question head in this section. Then use a different colour to highlight the answers to the questions.

Reading Check

1. What happens to the volume of matter when it expands?

_____

_____

_____

What is matter?

Mass is the amount of material that makes up an object. **Volume** is the amount of space that a material takes up. Anything that has mass and volume is called **matter.**

What are the states of matter?

The three common states of matter are solid, liquid, and gas. A solid has a distinct volume and shape. A liquid has a distinct volume and a shape that depends on the shape of its container. The volume and the shape of a gas depend on the size and shape of its container.

What happens to matter when its temperature changes?

When you add energy to matter, its temperature rises. This causes matter to expand. **Expansion** is an increase in the volume of something when its temperature rises. For instance, if the temperature of the air in a balloon rises, the volume of the air increases. The balloon gets a bit bigger.

When you take energy away from matter, its temperature falls. This causes matter to contract. **Contraction** is a decrease in the volume of something when its temperature falls. If you lower the temperature of the air in a balloon, the volume of the air decreases. The balloon gets a bit smaller.

If the temperature of matter keeps rising or falling, the state of the matter can change. The table on the next page shows how the state of matter changes. ✔

State of matter	Change of state when you add enough energy (raise the temperature)	Change of state when you take away enough energy (lower the temperature)
solid	**melting**: changes from solid to the liquid **sublimation**: changes from solid directly to gas	no change of state (stays solid)
liquid	**evaporation**: changes from liquid to gas	**solidification**: changes from liquid to solid
gas	no change of state (stays a gas)	**condensation**: changes from gas to liquid **deposition:** changes from gas directly to solid

Why does matter change volume or state?

Matter is made up of tiny particles. The particles have kinetic energy. This means they are always moving.

◆ Particles of a solid are packed close together. They are so close that they cannot move freely. They can only vibrate.

◆ Particles of a liquid are spaced a bit farther apart. They can slide past each other.

◆ Particles of a gas are spaced very far apart. They move around quickly.

The kinetic molecular theory explains how these particles act when energy is added or removed. When energy is added to particles, they move faster. This makes them move farther apart, and the matter expands. When energy is removed from particles, they move more slowly. This brings them closer together, and the matter contracts.

Adding energy to a solid can make its particles move faster and far enough apart for it to become a liquid. Adding energy to a liquid can make the particles move faster and far enough apart for it to become a gas. ✔

✓ Reading Check

2. Explain what happens to the particles of a solid as it changes to a liquid.

_____

_____

_____

Use with textbook pages 246–253.

Solids, liquids, and gases

Complete the following table to describe three states of matter. The table has been partially completed to help you.

	Solid	Liquid	Gas
shape		not fixed; takes the shape of the container	
volume	fixed volume		
spaces between particles			
movement of particles			can move freely and quickly in all directions in the container

In each of the jars below draw the particles in a gas, a liquid, and a solid. Make sure to indicate whether the particles are moving or vibrating in your diagrams.

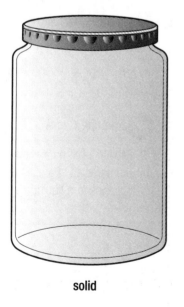

solid

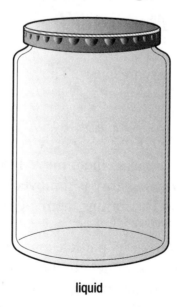

liquid

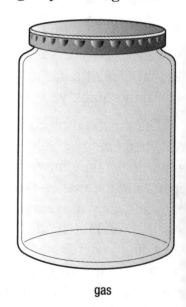

gas

Use with textbook pages 246–253.

Expand and contract

Vocabulary	
condensation	melting
contracts	move around quickly
deposition	rises
evaporation	slide past each other
expands	slower
falls	solidification
faster	state of matter
kinetic molecular theory	sublimation
mass	vibrate
matter	volume

Use the terms in the vocabulary box to fill in the blanks. Use each term only once. You do not need to use all the terms.

1. _____ is the amount of material that makes up something. _____ is the amount of space that a material takes up. Anything that has mass and volume is called _____.

2. When you add energy to matter, its temperature _____.

3. _____ is the process of a solid changing to a liquid. _____ is the process of a solid changing directly to a gas.

4. _____ is the process of a liquid changing to a gas. _____ is the process of a liquid changing to a solid.

5. _____ is the process of a gas changing to a liquid. _____ is the process of a gas changing to a solid.

6. Particles in a solid are packed so close together they can only _____. Particles in a liquid can _____. Particles in a gas can _____.

7. When you remove energy from particles they move _____ and the matter _____.

8. The _____ explains how particles act when their spacing and movement change.

Use with textbook pages 246–253.

What's the matter?

Vocabulary	
condensation	melting
deposition	solidification
evaporation	sublimation

Use the terms in the vocabulary box to label the diagram. Place the terms on the numbered arrows.

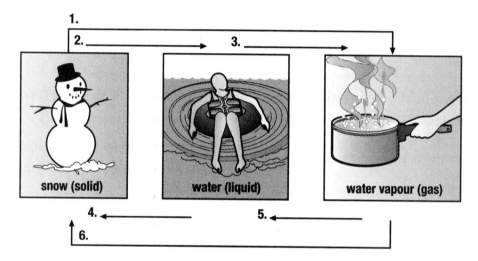

Complete the following table by describing the change of state. The table has been partially completed to help you.

	Change of state	Heat added or released
condensation		released
deposition		
evaporation	liquid to gas	
melting		added
solidification		
sublimation		

se with textbook pages 246–253.

tates of matter

Match each Term on the left with the best Descriptor on the right. Each Descriptor may be used only once.

Term	Descriptor
1. _____ mass 2. _____ matter 3. _____ volume	**A.** amount of matter in an object **B.** amount of space an object takes up **C.** anything that has mass and volume **D.** total energy of the particles in an object

Circle the letter of the best answer.

4. Which of the following is not an example of matter?

A. heat

B. solids

C. water

D. oxygen

5. What does the kinetic molecular theory explain?

A. how particles act when their spacing and movement change

B. how to determine the mass and volume of solids, liquids, and gases

C. how the kinetic energy in solids, liquids, and gases can be measured

D. how to find out the temperature of solids, liquids, and gases

6. What happens to matter when energy is added to it?

A. the particles take up less space

B. the particles decrease in volume

C. the particles move around faster

D. the particles move around slower

Use the following diagram to answer questions 7 to 9.

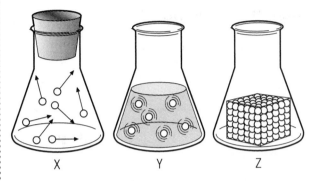

X   Y   Z

7. Both Y and Z have definite volume.

A. The statement is true.

B. The statement is false.

C. You cannot tell from the diagram.

8. The particles in Z can flow past each other.

A. The statement is true.

B. The statement is false.

C. You cannot tell from the diagram.

9. Which of the following correctly compares the amount of energy in the particles of X and Z?

A. The particles in X have less energy than the particles in Z.

B. The particles in X have more energy than the particles in Z.

C. The particles in both X and Z have the same amount of energy.

D. You cannot tell from the diagram.

Fluids and Density

Textbook pages 260–271

Before You Read

Why does a hot air balloon rise up in the air? Record your ideas on the lines below.

_____

_____

Mark the Text

Summarize
As you read this section, highlight the main point in each paragraph. Then write a short paragraph summarizing what you have learned.

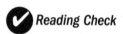

Reading Check

1. Explain what density is by comparing the particles of a gas with the particles of a liquid.

_____

_____

_____

What are fluids?

A **fluid** is any form of matter that can flow. Liquids and gases are fluids. They flow because they do not have a fixed shape. Solids are not fluids because they have a fixed, rigid shape.

Why are gases less dense than liquids?

The amount of mass that is contained in a certain volume of material is called **density**. Density describes the spacing of the particles in a material. For example, the particles of a gas are spaced very far apart. The particles of a liquid are spaced much closer together. A gas is less dense than a liquid because there is much more space between the particles in a gas than there is in a liquid.

In most cases, the liquid state of a substance is less dense than the solid state of the same substance. One exception is water. In solid water (ice), the particles are spaced farther apart than they are in liquid water. That is why ice floats on liquid water.

How can you compare the density of liquids?

Less dense liquids float on top of denser liquids. For example, olive oil is less dense than water. If you add olive oil and water to a glass, the olive oil would float on top of the water.

How does temperature affect density?

You know that the particles of a substance spread out more as the temperature rises. This means that a substance gets less dense as energy is added to it. Think of a hot air balloon. As energy is added to the air inside the balloon, the heated air gets less dense than the air outside the balloon. That is why a hot air balloon floats.

Name

Date

Section
7.2
Summary

continued

How do you find the density of an object?

Density is the amount of mass in a given volume. This means that you can find the density of a substance if you know its mass and its volume.

To measure the *mass* of a solid object, you use a balance. Measuring the *volume* of a solid object depends on its shape.

◆ If the object has a simple shape, for example a block, you can use math to find its volume. For a block, you multiply the length of the block by its width and by its height.

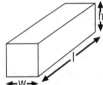

volume of a block = length × width × height

◆ If the object has an irregular shape, for example a juice bottle, you use a technique called displacement. **Displacement** is the amount of space that an object takes up when it is placed in a fluid. The amount of fluid that is displaced by an object is equal to the volume of the object. So if you put a bottle into a pail of water, and if 25 mL of water spill out (are displaced) from the pail, the volume of the bottle is 25 mL. ✔

How do you find density if you know the mass and the volume?

Density equals the mass of something divided by its volume. In other words:

density $(D) = \dfrac{\text{mass } (m)}{\text{volume } (V)}$ or $D = \dfrac{m}{V}$

The mass units for solids, liquids, and gases are often grams (g) or kilograms (kg). If the object is a solid, the volume units are often cubic centimetres (cm^3). For example, a a density of 11 g/cm^3. Water has a density of 1 g/mL.

If the object is a fluid, the volume units are often millilitres (mL).

✔ **Reading Check**

2. How would you use displacement to find the volume of a solid?

_____

_____

_____

Use textbook pages 260–265.

Go with the flow

Vocabulary	
cubic centimetres (cm³)	g/mL
denser	mass
density	millilitres (mL)
displacement	particles
float	rise
fluids	volume
g/cm³	water

Use the terms in the vocabulary box to fill in the blanks. Use each vocabulary term once only. You will not need to use every term.

1. _____ can flow because they do not have a fixed shape.

2. The _____ of an object is the amount of mass contained in a given volume.

3. The key to density is the spaces between the _____ The denser an object is, the more closely packed together the particles are in the object.

4. A less dense substance will _____ on a denser substance if the two substances do not mix together.

5. As a rule, substances are _____ in their solid state than in their liquid state. An exception to this rule is _____.

6. To calculate the density of an object, you need to divide its _____ by its _____.

7. The _____ method can be used to find the volume of an irregularly-shaped object.

8. The units for density can be _____ or _____.

Use with textbook pages 260–265.

Dense, denser, densest

Complete and label the diagrams according to the instructions below.

1. The table below lists the densities of five different fluids. If the fluids were added to a beaker, how would they be layered? Draw and label the layers in the beaker below.

Substance	Density (g/mL)
gasoline	0.69
glycerol	1.26
corn syrup	1.40
vegetable oil	0.92
rubbing alcohol	0.79

2. Water has a density of 1.00 g/mL. Draw and label each of the following objects in the tank of water. Show whether they will sink or float.

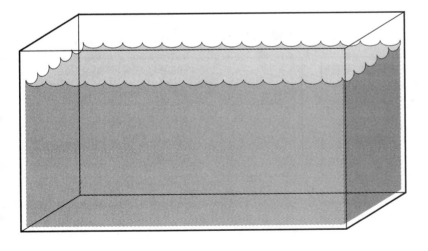

Object	Density
cork	0.24 g/cm^3
ice	0.92 g/cm^3
gold ring	19.32 g/cm^3
block of wood	0.66 g/cm^3
marble	2.5 g/cm^3

Use textbook pages 264–265.

Density detective

Use your detective skills to find the identity of the mystery objects. First calculate the density of the object. Then use the Table of Densities to decide what the object is made of.

Table of Densities

Solids	Density (g/cm³)	Solids	Density (g/cm³)
marble	2.56	copper	8.92
quartz	2.64	gold	19.32
diamond	3.52	platinum	21.4

1. While digging in the backyard, you find an old coin. Its mass is 26.76 g and its volume is 3 cm³. What is the density of the coin?

Calculation:

What is the coin made of? _____

2. You think you have found a diamond. Its mass is 5.28 g, and its volume is 2 cm³. What is the density of the object?

Calculation:

What did you find? _____

3.  You find a ring with a mass of 107 g. You fill a graduated cylinder up with 10 mL of water and put the ring into the cylinder. The water rises up to the 15 mL mark. What is the density of the ring?

Calculation:

What is the ring made of? _____

4. 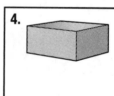 There is a block on your desk that acts as a paperweight. Its measurements are: 3 cm by 4 cm by 6 cm. The block has a mass of 184.32 g. What is the density of the block?

Calculation:

What is the block made of? _____

Use with textbook pages 260–265.

Fluids and density

Match each Substance/Object on the left with its Density. Each Density may be used only once.

Substance/Object	Density
1. _____ An object has a mass of 12 g and a volume of 2 cm³. Determine its density.	**A.** 6 cm³
	B. 6 g
	C. 6 g/ cm³
	D. 12 mL
2. _____ A substance has a mass of 24 g and a volume of 2 mL. Determine its density.	**E.** 12 g
	F. 12 g/mL

Circle the letter of the best answer.

3. Which of the following are fluids?

  A. gases only

  B. liquids only

  C. gases and liquids only

  D. solids, liquids, and gases

4. Why are fluids able to flow?

  A. they do not have a fixed shape

  B. they do not have a fixed volume

  C. their particles are packed tightly together

  D. their particles have very little kinetic energy

5. How would you determine the volume of an irregularly-shaped rock?

  A. Put the rock on a triple beam balance.

  B. Determine the density of the object and divide it by its mass.

  C. Use a ruler to measure its length, width, and height. Then multiply the dimensions together.

  D. Put the rock in a graduated cylinder filled with water and see how much water is displaced.

6. A graduated cylinder containing 50 mL of water has a mass of 70 g. As you put the object into the graduated cylinder, the water rises to 80 mL and the total mass increases to 90 g. What is the mass, volume, and density of the object?

  A. m = 20 g; V = 10 mL; D = 2 g/mL

  B. m = 20 g; V = 30 mL; D = 1.5 g/mL

  C. m = 20 g; V = 30 mL; D = 0.6 g/mL

  D. m = 30 g; V = 20 mL; D = 1.5 g/mL

Use the following diagrams to answer questions 7 to 9.

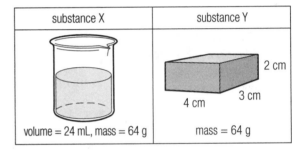

substance X	substance Y
volume = 24 mL, mass = 64 g	mass = 64 g

(substance Y: 2 cm, 3 cm, 4 cm)

7. The volume of substance Y is 24 cm³.

  A. The statement is true.

  B. The statement is false.

  C. There is not enough information to determine the density.

8. Which of the following compares the density of substance X and substance Y?

  A. Substance X is denser than substance Y.

  B. Substance Y is denser than substance X.

  C. Both substances have the same density.

9. If substance Y is placed in a beaker of water, what will happen?

  A. Substance Y will sink in water.

  B. Substance Y will float on water.

  C. Substance Y will dissolve in water.

Forces

Textbook pages 276–289

Before You Read

You push on a small boulder and it does not move. If you push with the help of a few friends, the boulder moves. What makes the difference? Write your ideas below.

_____

_____

Make Flash Cards

For each paragraph, think of a question that could be on a test. Write the question on one side of a flash card. Write the answer on the other side. Quiz yourself until you can answer all the questions.

⊘ Reading Check

1. What is the difference between a contact force and an action-at-a-distance force?

   _____

   _____

   _____

   _____

   _____

What is a force?

A **force** is a push or a pull that acts on an object. A force can cause an object to move or change. For instance:

◆ A force can set a motionless object in motion or make a moving object stop.

◆ A force can make a moving object slow down, speed up, or change direction.

◆ A force can change the shape of an object.

What types of forces are there?

You can group forces into two main types, contact forces and action-at-a-distance forces. Contact forces have an effect only on objects that they touch. Examples of contact forces:

◆ **Friction** works to slow down or stop motion due to surfaces rubbing against each other.

◆ Tension force is experienced by a rope when it is pulled at either end.

◆ Elastic force is exerted when a spring returns to its normal shape after being stretched.

Action-at-a-distance forces act on objects without touching them. Examples of action-at-a-distance forces:

◆ **Gravitation** pulls objects toward each other. A ball that is tossed in the air falls to the ground because of this force.

◆ **Magnetic** force pulls or pushes on metals and compounds such as iron, nickel, and cobalt.

◆ Static electricity, such as in lightning, causes pushing and pulling forces. ✔

How are forces measured?

Force is measured in units called newtons. It takes about one newton (1 N) of force to lift or to hold up the mass of a medium apple against the force of gravity.

The newton is related to the weight of an object. **Weight** is the amount of force that gravity exerts on the mass of an object. This means that weight is not the same as mass. The mass of an object measures the amount of matter in it. The weight of an object measures how strongly gravity pulls on that amount of matter. Gravity pulls more strongly on objects that have more mass. ✔

What happens when forces are balanced and unbalanced?

Balanced forces are forces that are equal in size and act in opposite directions. If balanced forces act on an object that is not moving, it will not move. If the object is moving, it will keep moving in the same direction and at the same speed.

Unbalanced forces are not equal in size. They do not have to act in opposite directions. If unbalanced forces act on an object that is not moving, it can move. The movement is in the direction of the stronger force.

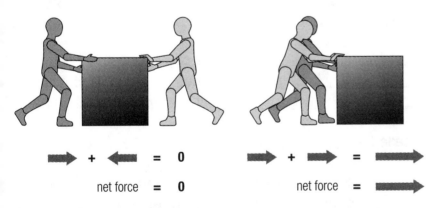

These forces are balanced. They are equal in size (amount of force), and they act in opposite directions. The box does not move.

These forces are unbalanced. They are not equal in size. The box moves in the direction of the stronger force.

✔ Reading Check

2. How is weight different from mass?

_____

_____

_____

Name _____   Date _____

Use with textbook pages 276–285.

What is a force?

Vocabulary	
action-at-a-distance	magnetic
balanced	mass
can	newtons
contact	static electricity
elastic	tension
force	unbalanced
friction	volume
grams	weight
gravitation	will not

Use the terms in the vocabulary box to fill in the blanks. Each term may be used only once. You will not need to use all the terms.

1. A(n) _____ is a push or a pull that acts on an object.

2. _____ forces only have an effect on objects that they touch. _____ forces act on an object without touching it.

3. _____ works to slow down or stop motion due to surfaces rubbing against each other. _____ force is experienced by a rope when it is pulled at either end. _____ force is exerted when a spring returns to its normal shape.

4. A(n) _____ force pulls objects toward each other. A(n) _____ force pulls or pushes on metals such as iron. _____ causes pushing and pulling forces.

5. Force is measured in units called _____.

6. The _____ of an object measures the amount of matter in it. The _____ of an object measures how strongly gravity pulls on that amount of matter.

7. _____ forces are forces that are equal in size and act in opposite directions.

8. _____ forces are not equal in size. They do not have to act in opposite directions.

Use with textbook pages 276–285.

Name the force

On the first blank line, state what type of force is illustrated in the picture.

Choose from the following list: tension, friction, elastic, gravitational, static electricity, magnetic.

On the second blank line, state whether it is a contact force or an action-at-a-distance force.

1.

The trampoline stretches.

_____

_____

2.

A person parachutes from the sky.

_____

_____

3.

A magnet collects the iron nails.

_____

_____

4.

A rain cloud produces lightning.

_____

_____

Use with textbook pages 276–285.

True or false?

Read the statements given below. If the statement is true, write "T" on the line in front of the statement. If it is false, write "F" and rewrite the statement to make it true.

1. _____ A force cannot set a motionless object in motion.

_____

2. _____ A force can make a moving object change direction.

_____

3. _____ A force can change the shape of an object.

_____

4. _____ Tension force slows down or stops motion due to surfaces rubbing against each other.

_____

5. _____ Elastic force pulls objects toward each other.

_____

6. _____ An example of magnetic force is lightning.

_____

7. _____ The weight of an object measures how strongly friction pulls on that amount of matter.

_____

8. _____ Force is measured in units called newtons.

_____

9. _____ Balanced forces are forces that are equal in size and act in opposite directions.

_____

10. _____ If unbalanced forces act on an object that is not moving, it can move.

_____

Use with textbook pages 276–285.

Forces

Match the Term on the left with the best Descriptor on the right. Each Descriptor may be used only once.	
Term	**Descriptor**
1. _____ elastic **2.** _____ tension **3.** _____ friction **4.** _____ magnetic **5.** _____ static electricity **6.** _____ gravitation	**A.** an apple falls from a tree branch **B.** a person uses a rope to pull a friend on a sled **C.** a magnet holds a picture on a fridge **D.** a person pulls a bow back and shoots the arrow **E.** a sock is stuck to a sweater as it comes out of the dryer **F.** when a person stops pedalling, the bicycle slows down

Circle the letter of the best answer.

7. What is a force?

 A. a push or a pull

 B. the amount of mass in an object

 C. the amount of matter in an object

 D. the amount of pressure an object has

8. Which of the following describes what a force can do?

I.	move or stop an object
II.	change the shape of an object
III.	change the direction of a moving object

 A. I and II only

 B. I and III only

 C. II and III only

 D. I, II, and III

9. What are two categories into which all forces can be placed?

 A. contact forces and balanced forces

 B. unbalanced forces and gravitational forces

 C. contact forces and action-at-a-distance forces

 D. balanced forces and action-at-a-distance forces

10. Which of the following is not a contact force?

 A. elastic

 B. tension

 C. friction

 D. static electricity

11. A person runs a lot slower on sand than on pavement. What type of force is responsible for this?

 A. elastic

 B. tension

 C. friction

 D. static electricity

12. You rub a balloon on your head and as you pull the balloon away your hair starts to stand up. What force causes your hair to be attracted to the balloon?

 A. elastic

 B. tension

 C. static electricity

 D. gravitation

13. What is a newton a unit for?

 A. mass

 B. force

 C. density

 D. volume

Pressure

Textbook pages 290–299

Before You Read

What do you think pressure is? What might happen if you apply pressure to a solid, liquid, or gas? Write your ideas in the lines below.

_____

_____

 Mark the Text

In Your Own Words
Highlight the main idea in each paragraph. Stop after each paragraph and put what you just read into your own words.

 *Reading Check*

1. Why can you compress a gas but not a liquid or a solid?

   _____

   _____

   _____

What is pressure?

Pressure is the amount of force that acts on a given area of an object. Think about writing with a sharp pencil and a dull pencil. Which puts more pressure on the paper if you press down with the same amount of force? The sharp pencil does. It concentrates the force into a smaller area than does the dull pencil.

How does pressure affect matter?

Pressure can cause a gas to be compressed. Picture the particles of air inside a balloon. Air is a gas, so its particles are spread far apart. What happens if you squeeze or press down on the balloon? Its shape changes. This happens because the increased pressure on the balloon pushes the air particles closer together. As a result, the air in the balloon takes up a smaller volume. In other words, the balloon is compressed. **Compression** is a decrease in the volume of matter caused by a force.

Gases are easy to compress, because the particles of a gas are spread far apart. What about liquids and solids? The particles that make up liquids and solids are very close together. There is little room to push them closer to decrease their volume. So liquids and solids normally do not compress very much. ✔

What happens when a gas-filled container explodes?

The particles of a gas move faster and farther apart when energy is added. As a result, the gas expands. If the heated gas is trapped inside a container, the gas particles bounce against the sides faster and more often. This means that the heated gas exerts more pressure on the inside of the container. This added pressure can lead to an explosion.

How is pressure measured?

Recall that pressure is the amount of force on an area. You can write this as a formula:

$$\text{pressure } (P) = \frac{\text{force } (F)}{\text{area } (A)}, \text{ or } P = \frac{F}{A}$$

What units are used for F (force) and A (area)? Recall from section 8.1 that force is measured in newtons (N). Recall that area is often measured in square metres (m^2). Pressure is measured in units of newtons per square metre, or N/m^2.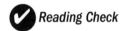

A pressure that is equal to 1 N/m^2 is called a **pascal**, which has the symbol Pa (1 Pa = 1 N/m^2). This is a very small amount of pressure. Therefore, pressure is often measured using a unit equal to 1000 Pa. This unit is called a **kilopascal**. It has the symbol kPa (1 kPa = 1000 Pa).

✅ **Reading Check**

2. What is the formula for pressure?

_____

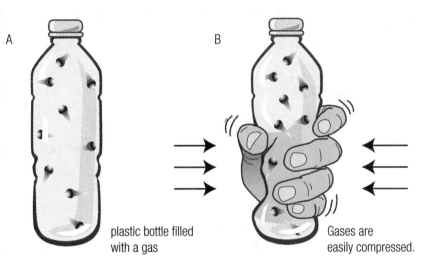

A · plastic bottle filled with a gas

B · Gases are easily compressed.

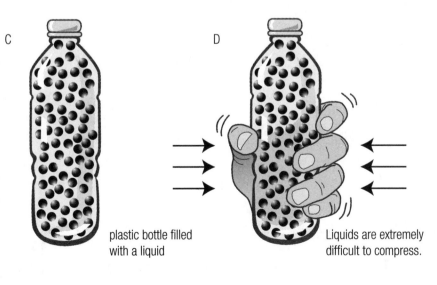

C · plastic bottle filled with a liquid

D · Liquids are extremely difficult to compress.

Use with textbook pages 290–296.

What is pressure?

Vocabulary	
area	liquids
compression	m²
decreases	N
explosion	N/m²
force	Pa
gases	pascal
increases	pressure
kilopascal	solids
kPa	volume

Use the terms in the vocabulary box to fill in the blanks. You can use the terms more than once. You will not need to use every term.

1. _____ is the amount of force that acts on a given area of an object.

2. _____ is a decrease in the volume of matter caused by a force. Pressure can cause a gas to be compressed. As a result, the volume of the gas _____.

3. _____ are easy to compress, because their particles are spread far apart.

4. If the heated gas is trapped inside a container, the gas particles bounce against the sides faster and more often. This means that the heated gas exerts more _____ on the inside of the container. This added pressure can lead to a(n)_____.

5. In the formula $P = \frac{F}{A}$, P stands for_____, F stands for_____, and A stands for _____.

6. Force is measured in _____.
   Area is often measured in _____.

7. A pressure that is equal to 1 N/m² is called a_____.
   It has the symbol _____.

8. Pressure is often measured in units 1000 Pa, which is called a _____.
   It has the symbol _____.

Use with textbook pages 290–296

Compression

Draw diagrams to help explain the statements below. Show what is happening to the particles in the substances described. Label your diagrams.

1. It is fairly easy to compress a balloon partly filled with air.

2. A sealed can containing a heated gas explodes when the gas inside is heated.

Use with textbook pages 290–296.

Under some pressure

The formula for pressure is $P = \dfrac{F}{A}$

The formula for area is $A = l \times w$

Calculate the pressure for each example below. Show all your work, including the formula(s) that you use.

1.

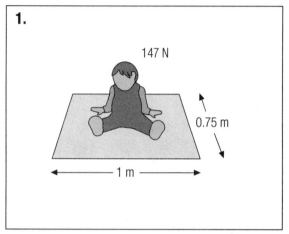

147 N

0.75 m

1 m

Calculations:

2.

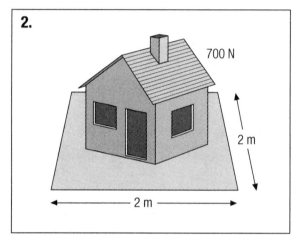

700 N

2 m

2 m

Calculations:

3.

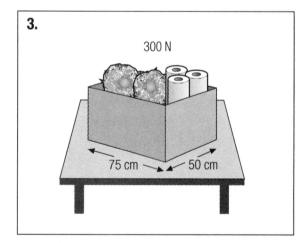

300 N

75 cm   50 cm

Calculations:

4.

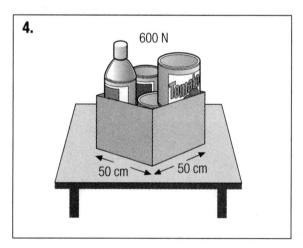

600 N

50 cm   50 cm

Calculations:

Use with textbook pages 290–296.

Pressure

Match the Unit on the left with the Term that it measures on the right. Each Term may be used as often as necessary.

Unit	Term
1. _____ pascal (Pa)	**A.** area
2. _____ newton (N)	**B.** force
3. _____ kilopascal (kPa)	**C.** length
4. _____ metre (m)	**D.** pressure
5. _____ square metre (m^2)	
6. _____ square centimetre (cm^2)	

Circle the letter of the best answer.

7. Which of the following describes what happens to the particles of air inside a bottle as pressure is applied?

A. the particles will speed up

B. the particles will slow down

C. the particles will move farther apart

D. the particles will move closer together

8. What is compression?

A. a decrease in mass produced by a force

B. an increase in mass produced by a force

C. a decrease in volume produced by a force

D. an increase in volume produced by a force

9. Why can a gas be easily compressed?

A. it has no fixed shape

B. it has no fixed volume

C. its particles have a lot of kinetic energy

D. it has a large amount of space between its particles

10. What states of matter are not easily compressible?

I.	gas
II.	solid
III.	liquid

A. I and II only

B. I and III only

C. II and III only

D. I, II, and III

11. What will happen to the pressure if the force is decreased?

A. the pressure will increase

B. the pressure will also decrease

C. the pressure will stay the same

D. it depends on the type of force

12. Calculate the amount of pressure exerted by a large wooden crate that weighs 1200 N and has a base with dimensions 4 m by 4 m.

A. 0.013 Pa

B. 75 Pa

C. 150 Pa

D. 300 Pa

13. What is pressure?

A. the change in volume produced by a force

B. the change in mass produced by a force

C. the amount of compression placed on an object

D. the amount of force that acts on a given area of an object

Viscosity, Adhesion, and Cohesion

Textbook pages 300–309

Before You Read

Motor oil from a hot engine flows more easily than motor oil from a cold engine. Why is there a difference? Write your ideas on the lines below.

_____

_____

Create an Outline
Make an outline of the information in this section. Use the headings in the reading as a starting point. Include the bold terms and any other terms that you think are important.

✔ *Reading Check*

1. Which liquid has a greater viscosity at room temperature: honey or water? Explain why.

_____

_____

_____

What is viscosity?

Some fluids are thicker or thinner than others. For instance, water is thinner than honey. Molasses is thicker than vegetable oil.

The thinness or thickness of a liquid is a property of fluids called viscosity. **Viscosity** describes a fluid's resistance to flow—that is, how difficult it is for the fluid to flow. A thick liquid has a greater viscosity than a thin liquid. The thicker liquid is more resistant to flow. Therefore, it flows more slowly than a thinner liquid. ✔

How do heating and cooling affect viscosity?

To compare the viscosity of fluids, you can measure their flow rate. The **flow rate** of a fluid is the speed at which a fluid flows from one point to another. The flow rate of honey is slower than the flow rate of water. Why? Honey is more viscous (has a greater viscosity) than water.

What happens if honey is heated? The particles that make up honey move farther apart. Now the honey is less viscous than it was before. Heating a liquid decreases its viscosity. Cooling a liquid increases its viscosity.

What happens when a gas is heated? The particles that make up the gas move faster and collide more often when the gas is heated. Heating a gas increases its viscosity. Cooling a gas decreases its viscosity.

Liquids				
heated ➡	particles further apart ➡	less attraction between particles ➡	less friction ➡	viscosity decreases
cooled ➡	particles closer together ➡	increased attraction between particles ➡	more friction ➡	viscosity increases
Gases				
heated ➡	particles further apart ➡	particles move faster ➡	more collisions, so more friction ➡	viscosity increases
cooled ➡	particles closer together ➡	particles move slower ➡	fewer collisions, so less friction ➡	viscosity decreases

The effects of adding and removing heat on the viscosity of fluids are shown above.

What is cohesion?

Suppose you put a drop of water on a flat sheet of plastic. The water drop takes the shape of a disc. Why does it hold this shape? The particles that make up water are attracted to each other and tend to cling together. The property of fluids that makes the particles hold together because they are attracted to each other is called **cohesion**.

The water particles at the surface attract each other in a way that makes the surface act like a skin. This effect is called **surface tension**. Picture a compact disc (CD) and a large bowl of water. The CD is denser than water, so it should sink. If you drop the compact disc edgewise into the water, the CD does sink. If you rest the compact disc gently on the surface of the water, what happens? It floats! This happens because of surface tension of the water.

What is adhesion?

Have you ever seen drops of rain or dew perched on the edge of a leaf? You may have seen this same effect with drops of water that cling to the side of a glass. This property of water and other fluids is called adhesion. **Adhesion** is the attraction between particles of a fluid and another substance so that the fluid clings to it. ✔

✔ **Reading Check**

2. Explain how cohesion and adhesion are different.

_____

_____

_____

Use with textbook pages 300–305.

Properties of fluids

Vocabulary	
adhesion	heated
cohesion	increases
decreases	slowly
faster	surface tension
flow rate	thicker
fluid	thinner
greater	viscosity

Use the terms in the vocabulary box to fill in the blanks. You can use each vocabulary term more than once. You will not need to use every term.

1. A(n) _____ is any substance that flows.

2. The thinness or thickness of a fluid is a property of fluids called _____. For instance, water is _____ than honey. Molasses is _____ than vegetable oil.

3. A thick fluid has a _____ viscosity than a thin fluid. The thicker fluid is more resistant to flow. Therefore, it flows more _____ than a thinner fluid.

4. To compare the viscosity of fluids, you can measure their _____, which is the speed at which fluid flows from one point to another.

5. Heating a liquid _____ its viscosity.

6. Heating a gas _____ its viscosity.

7. The property of fluids that makes the particles hold together because they are attracted to each other is called _____.

8. The water particles at the surface attract each other in a way that makes the surface act like a skin. This effect is called _____.

9. The attraction between particles of a fluid and another substance so that the fluid clings to it is called _____.

se with textbook pages 300–305.

Viscosity of different substances

Data has been collected from an experiment investigating how temperature affects the iscosity of three substances.

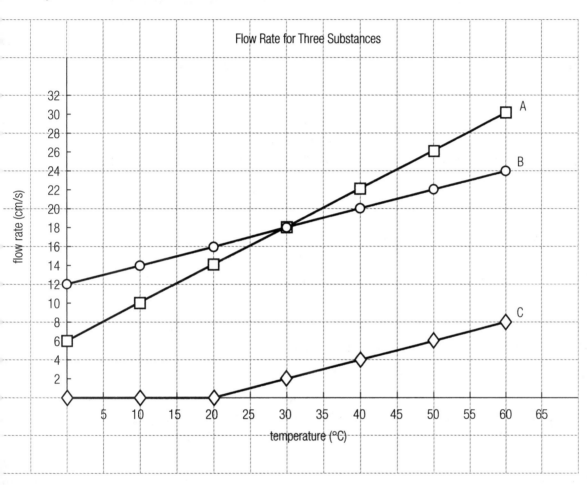

Use the data in the graph above to answer the questions below.

1. Which substance is a solid at room temperature (about 20°C)? _____

2. At what temperature is the viscosity of substance A and substance B equal?

_____

3. When the temperature is 20°C, which substance has the greatest flow rate?

_____

4. When the temperature is 50°C, which substance has the greatest flow rate?

_____

5. Suppose that substance A was at 65°C. Use your graph to predict how fast substance A would flow. _____

Use with textbook pages 300–305.

How does it flow?

Complete the diagram below by giving a definition, listing some characteristics, and providing examples and non-examples of viscous (thick) liquids. Some examples are already given to guide you.

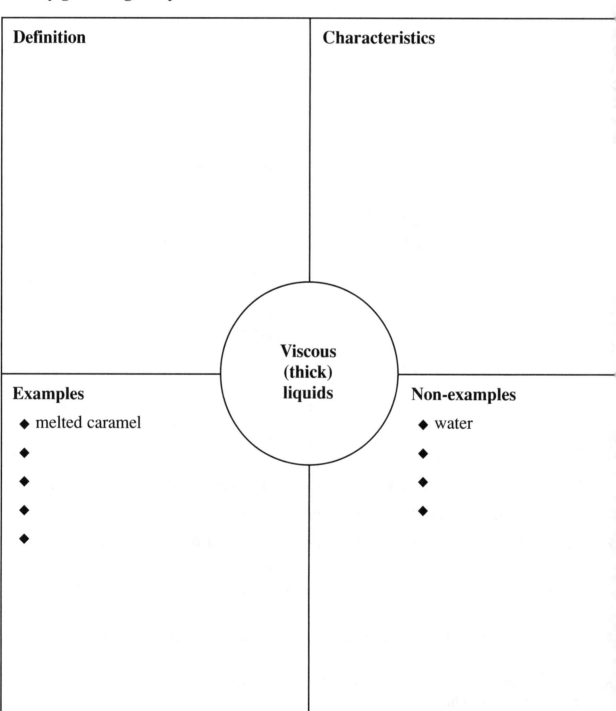

Definition

Characteristics

Viscous
(thick)
liquids

Examples
◆ melted caramel
◆
◆
◆
◆

Non-examples
◆ water
◆
◆
◆

se with textbook pages 300–305.

Viscosity, adhesion, and cohesion

Match the Term on the left with the best Descriptor on the right. Each Descriptor may be used only once.

Term	Descriptor
1. _____ cohesion 2. _____ adhesion 3. _____ viscosity 4. _____ flow rate 5. _____ surface tension	**A.** resistance to flow **B.** the speed at which a fluid flows from one point to another **C.** attraction or joining of two different objects or fluids to each other **D.** strength with which the particles of an object or fluid attract each other **E.** property of a liquid in which the surface of the liquid acts like a thin skin

Circle the letter of the best answer.

6. Which of the following explains how the viscosity of a fluid is related to its flow rate?

A. as the viscosity of a fluid decreases, its flow rate increases

B. as the viscosity of a fluid increases, its flow rate also increases

C. as the viscosity of a fluid decreases, its flow rate also decreases

D. as the viscosity of a fluid decreases, its flow rate stays the same

7. Which of the following has the greatest viscosity at room temperature?

A. water

B. milk

C. vegetable oil

D. molasses

8. Which of the following statements correctly describes the viscosity in a liquid?

I.	As a liquid is heated, the viscosity increases.
II.	As a liquid is heated, the viscosity decreases.
III.	As a liquid is cooled, the viscosity increases.
IV.	As a liquid is cooled, the viscosity decreases.

A. I and III only

B. I and IV only

C. II and III only

D. II and IV only

9. Which of the following statements correctly describes the viscosity in a gas?

I.	As a gas is heated, the viscosity increases.
II.	As a gas is heated, the viscosity decreases.
III.	As a gas is cooled, the viscosity increases.
IV.	As a gas is cooled, the viscosity decreases.

A. I and III only

B. I and IV only

C. II and III only

D. II and IV only

10. Which of the following is an example of cohesion?

I.	a water strider walking on water
II.	a steel paper clip floating on water
III.	dewdrops on a spider web making rounded shapes

A. I only

B. III only

C. I and II only

D. I, II, and III

Fluids Under Pressure

Textbook pages 314–323

Before You Read

Which do you think is under greater pressure: a boat floating on top of water or a submarine exploring the ocean bottom? Explain your opinion below.

_____

_____

 **Mark the Text**

In Your Own Words
Highlight the main idea in each paragraph. Stop after each paragraph and put what you just read into your own words.

 **Reading Check**

1. Why does pressure in a fluid increase with depth?

_____

_____

_____

How does pressure in fluids change with depth?

Picture a tall, thin tube standing straight up and filled with water. Is the pressure of the water higher at the top of the tube or at the bottom? There is very little water pushing down on the water at the top of the tube. There is a lot more water pushing down on the water at the bottom of the tube. So the pressure at the bottom is higher.

Picture the same tall, thin tube again. This time, imagine it is filled with air instead of water. Is the pressure of the air higher at the top or at the bottom? There is a lot more air pushing down on the air at the bottom of the tube. The pressure of the air at the bottom is higher. For water, air, and all other fluids, pressure increases with depth. ✔

The pressure of air at sea level is called **one atmosphere** (1 atm). (One atmosphere is the same as 101.3 kPa.) With each 10 m that you go deeper in water than sea level, the pressure goes up by 1 atm. That might not sound like much, but 1 atm is a lot of pressure. It is the same as 10 000 kg pushing down on an area of 1 m^2, or 1 kg pushing down on an area of 1 cm^2.

What is buoyancy?

Buoyancy is the tendency for objects to rise or float in a fluid. Buoyancy occurs because of differences in density of the object and the fluid. Objects rise or float in a fluid because the fluid pushes up on them with a force, called the **buoyant force**. If this upward pushing force is greater than the downward pulling force of gravity on the object, the object rises or floats.

What is convection?

The buoyant force is what makes heated air rise. When air is heated, its particles move apart. The density of the heated air is less than the density of the cooler air around it. So the heated air rises. As this happens, denser, cooler air sinks to fill the space left by the heated air. This transfer of heat through the flow of a heated fluid is called **convection**.

Why do objects sink, rise, or float?

Examine the diagram below. When the buoyant force and the force of gravity are unbalanced (as they are in A and B), an object will move in the direction of the larger force. When the two forces are balanced (as in C), no motion will occur. ✔

A Sinking (for example, a rock in air)   **B** Rising (for example, a helium balloon in air)   **C** Floating (for example, a boat on water)

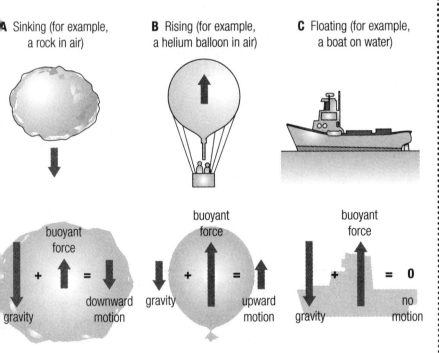

✔ Reading Check

2. If a boat sinks in water, which force is larger: gravity or buoyant force?

_____

_____

_____

Use with textbook pages 314–318.

All that pressure

Examine each figure, and then answer the questions.

1. Why is the fluid from the bottom hole forced out farther than the fluid from the top hole?

2. (a) Is the air pressure greater at the base of a mountain or the top of the mountain?

(b) Why?

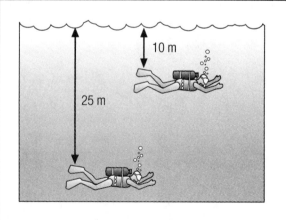

10 m

25 m

3. (a) There is 1 atm of pressure exerted on the diver at sea level. How much pressure is exerted on the diver at a depth of 10 m?

(b) How much pressure is exerted on the diver at a depth of 25 m?

se with textbook pages 314–318.

luid pressure

ompare the force arrows for each object. The larger the arrow, the more force it presents. State whether the object is sinking, rising, or floating.

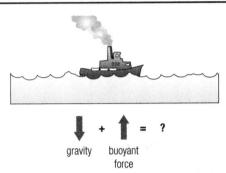

gravity　buoyant force

1. Is the boat rising, sinking, or floating?

_____

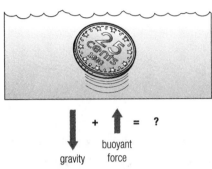

buoyant force

gravity

2. Is the coin rising, sinking, or floating?

_____

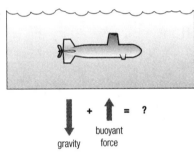

gravity buoyant force

3. Is the submarine rising, sinking, or floating?

_____

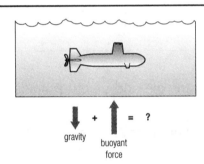

gravity buoyant force

4. Is the submarine rising, sinking, or floating?

_____

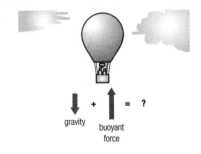

gravity buoyant force

5. Is the hot air balloon rising, sinking, or floating?

_____

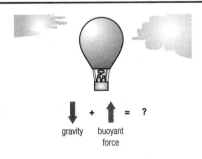

gravity buoyant force

6. Is the hot air balloon rising, sinking, or floating?

_____

Use with textbook pages 314–318.

Putting on the pressure

Vocabulary	
1 atm	float
10 atm	gravity
10 m	higher
buoyancy	increases
buoyant	lower
convection	pressure
decreases	rise
density	sink

Use the terms in the vocabulary box to fill in the blanks. You can use each term as many times as necessary. You will not need to use all the terms.

1. In a tube filled with water, the pressure is _____ at the top and _____ at the bottom.

2. In a tube filled with air, the pressure is _____ at the top and _____ at the bottom.

3. For water, air, and all other fluids, pressure _____ with depth.

4. The pressure of air at sea level is called _____.

5. With each 10 m that you go deeper in water than sea level, the pressure goes up by _____.

6. The tendency for objects to rise or float in a fluid is called _____

7. Buoyancy occurs because of differences in _____ of the object and the fluid.

8. Objects rise or float in a fluid because the fluid exerts a _____ force on them.

9. If the _____ force is greater than the force of _____ the object will rise.

10. If the buoyant force is equal to the force of _____ the object will _____.

Use with textbook pages 314–318.

Fluids under pressure

Match the Term on the left with the best Descriptor on the right. Each Descriptor may be used only once.	
Term	**Descriptor**
1. _____ buoyancy 2. _____ convection 3. _____ buoyant force 4. _____ gravitational force	A. pressure at sea level B. upward force exerted by a fluid C. downward force exerted by a fluid D. ability or tendency to rise or sink in a fluid E. heat transfer through the flow of a fluid

Circle the letter of the best answer.

5. When you are swimming underwater, why do you feel pressure of the water all around you?

   A. buoyant force is greater under water

   B. water particles are heavier than air particles

   C. there are more water particles than air particles

   D. the weight of all the water and the air above you pushes down on you

6. Which of the following is correct about fluid pressure?

   A. it remains the same at all depths

   B. it increases as the depth increases

   C. it increases as the depth decreases

   D. it decreases as the depth increases

Use the following diagram to answer question 7.

Barrel I   Barrel II

7. Notice that there is a hole on the side of each barrel. Assume both oil barrels are exactly the same and both are full with oil. Which of the following correctly compares oil flowing out of the oil barrels?

   A. Oil will be forced much farther from Barrel I than Barrel II.

   B. Oil will be forced much farther from Barrel II than Barrel I.

   C. Oil will be forced out the same distance from both barrels.

   D. The relationship cannot be determined from the information given.

Use the following diagram to answer question 8.

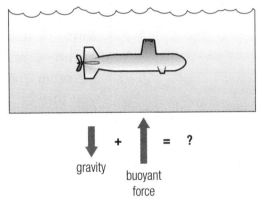

8. What will the submarine in the above diagram do?

   A. rise

   B. sink

   C. float

   D. none of the above

Constructed Fluid Systems

Textbook pages 324–333

Before You Read

What role does pressure play in getting water from its source to your sink? Record your ideas below.

_____

_____

 Mark the Text

Check for Understanding

As you read this section, be sure to reread any parts you do not understand. Highlight any sentence that helps you understand those parts.

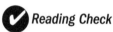 *Reading Check*

1. What is an example of a hydraulic system?

_____

_____

_____

What is a fluid system?

A fluid system is something that makes use of a gas or a liquid to perform tasks. If the fluid is a liquid, the system is hydraulic (high-DRAW-lik). If the fluid is a gas, the system is pneumatic (new-MAT-ik).

Fluid systems are all around you. The pipes that bring water to your home are part of a fluid system. A jackhammer that chips through pavement is also a fluid system.

What is a hydraulic system?

Hydraulics is the study of how liquids act when they are under pressure. A device that uses liquid under pressure to apply force in order to move something is called a **hydraulic system**. Most hydraulic systems apply a force on a liquid that fills a closed space, such as a tank or a pipe. The applied force creates pressure that moves the liquid through a series of tubes, pipes, or hoses. This causes motion of some kind at the other end of the system. You use a hydraulic system when you turn on a hose or a water tap. When you squeeze a tube of toothpaste, you are using a hydraulic system, too. ✔

Why do hydraulic systems often use a pump?

In many hydraulic systems, pumps are used to give the force that pushes the liquid. Pumps put the liquid under pressure. Think about the water you use at home. The pipes that bring water to your home are below the ground. The water must be put under pressure to move it against the force of gravity up to your sink. Putting a liquid under pressure means it can travel long distances. In a water pipe, you put the water under pressure at one end so you can get water out of the other end.

Mechanics depend on hydraulic systems to lift cars and other heavy objects. They use **hydraulic multiplication** to increase and transmit a force through a liquid from one place to another.

What is a pneumatic system?

Pneumatics is the study of how gases act when they are under pressure. A device that uses gas under pressure to apply a force in order to move something is called a **pneumatic system**. A pneumatic system uses a device called a compressor to compress the air so pressure builds up. When the pressure is released, the gas exerts a strong, steady force. This force can be used to fill tires, drill teeth, and bring heavy trucks to a safe stop through the use of air brakes. ●

What are some problems with hydraulic and pneumatic systems?

Hydraulic and pneumatic systems cannot work if they lose pressure. A crack or hole in a closed fluid-filled container (such as a pipe) will let fluid leak out and reduce pressure. Hydraulic and pneumatic systems cannot work if they become blocked. For example, if a vacuum cleaner filter becomes clogged with dust the vacuum will not work well.

✔ **Reading Check**

2. What is an example of a pneumatic system?

_____

_____

_____

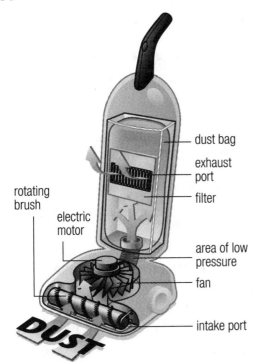

rotating brush

electric motor

dust bag

exhaust port

filter

area of low pressure

fan

intake port

DUST

Use with textbook pages 324–331.

Fluids at rest and fluids in motion

Vocabulary	
fluid	liquid
gas	pneumatics
hydraulics	pneumatic system
hydraulic system	pressure
hydraulic multiplication	pumps

Use the terms in the vocabulary box above to fill in the blanks. You can use each term as many times as necessary. You will not need to use all the terms.

1. A _____ system is something that makes use of a gas or a liquid to perform tasks.

2. The study of how liquids act when they are under pressure is called _____.

3. A device that uses pressure to apply a force through a liquid to move something else is called a _____.

4. You use a _____ when you turn on a hose or a water tap.

5. In many hydraulic systems, _____ are used to put the liquid under pressure.

6. The pipes that bring water to your home are below the ground. The water must be put under _____ to move it against the force of gravity up to your sink.

7. In a hydraulic system, you put a _____ under pressure so it can move something else at the other end.

8. Mechanics depend on hydraulic systems to lift cars and other heavy objects. They use _____ to increase and transmit a force through a liquid from one place to another.

9. The study of how gases act when they are under pressure is called _____.

10. A device that uses pressure to apply a force through a gas to move something else is called a _____.

Use with textbook pages 324–331.

Comparing systems

1. Use a Venn diagram to help you compare two concepts. On the left side of the Venn diagram, write the things that are only true of hydraulic systems. On the right side, write the things that are only true of pneumatic systems. In the middle, write the things that are true of both systems.

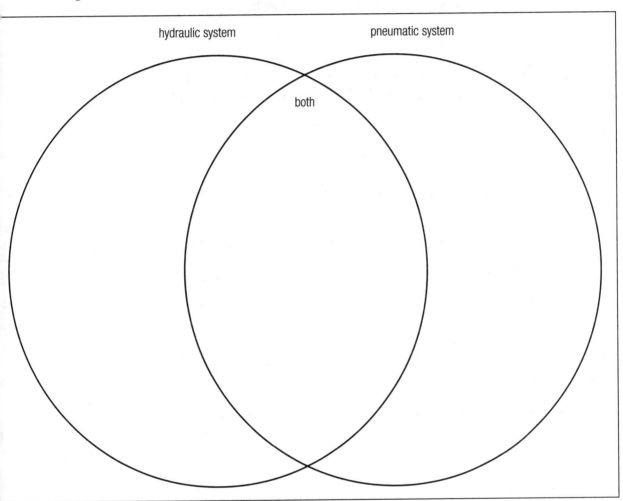

2. List two uses for each type of system.

   Hydraulic system:

   _____

   _____

   Pneumatic system:

   _____

   _____

Use with textbook pages 324–331.

True or false?

Read the statements given below. If the statement is true, write "T" on the line in front of the sentence. If it is false, write "F" and then rewrite the statement so it is true.

1. _____ Hydraulics is the study of pressure in solids.

_____

_____

2. _____ Hydraulic systems produce pressure that moves through a gas.

_____

_____

3. _____ Water usually flows downwards due to the force of gravity, but it can also flow upwards if it is placed under pressure.

_____

_____

4. _____ A hydraulic system uses a device to compress the air so pressure builds up.

_____

_____

5. _____ Pumps are important parts of pneumatic systems.

_____

_____

6. _____ Hydraulic multiplication is used to increase and transmit a force through a liquid from one place to another.

_____

_____

7. _____ Pneumatic systems use liquid in an enclosed system under pressure.

_____

_____

Use with textbook pages 324–331.

Constructed fluid systems

Match the Term on the left with the best Descriptor on the right. Each Descriptor may be used only once.	
Term	**Descriptor**
1. _____ hydraulics **2.** _____ pneumatics **3.** _____ hydraulic system **4.** _____ pneumatic system **5.** _____ hydraulic multiplication	**A.** a system in which an enclosed gas transmits a force, causing motion **B.** the study of pressure in liquids **C.** a device that transmits an applied force using a liquid under pressure **D.** the study of pressure in gases **E.** something that makes use of gas or liquid to perform tasks **F.** using a liquid to increase and transmit a force from one point to another

Circle the letter of the best answer.

6. Which of the following describes what happens when pressure is applied at one point to a fluid in an enclosed system?

A. that pressure is increased at the other end of the system

B. that pressure is decreased at the other end of the system

C. the pressure at the other end of the system does not change

D. you cannot apply pressure to a fluid in an enclosed system

7. Which of the following is created when an enclosed fluid is squeezed?

A. buoyancy

B. convection

C. pressure

D. gravity

8. Which of the following are usually important parts of hydraulic systems?

I.	pipes
II.	pumps
III.	compressors

A. II only

B. III only

C. I and II only

D. I, II, and III

9. What allows a pump to raise fluids in pipes?

A. area

B. force

C. gravity

D. pressure

10. Which of the following could cause a loss of pressure in a hydraulics system?

I.	a crack in a pipe
II.	a hole in pipe
III.	a blockage in a pipe

A. I and II only

B. II and III only

C. I and III only

D. I, II, and III

Natural Fluid Systems

Textbook pages 334–343

Before You Read

What fluid systems exist in nature? Write your thoughts below.

Mark the Text

Reinforce Your Understanding

As you read this section, highlight the main point of each paragraph. Use a different colour to highlight an example that helps explain the main point.

Reading Check

1. How is the circulatory system like a hydraulic system that people build?

_____

_____

_____

What are natural fluid systems?

There are many fluid systems that occur naturally, such as volcanoes and hurricanes. There are also natural fluid systems that are within your body.

How is the circulatory system a natural hydraulic system?

The **circulatory system** transports blood through the body. The circulatory system is made up of the heart, blood vessels, and blood. The constant beating of the heart (a pump) keeps blood moving through blood vessels (tubes or pipes). ✔

Blood must be kept under pressure so it can reach all parts of the body. Blood pressure increases and decreases between heartbeats. Just after the heart contracts, blood leaves the heart under high pressure. Before the next heart beat, the pressure falls. Then the pressure increases again as soon as the heart contracts again.

Blood pressure is measured with a **sphygmomanometer** (sfig-mom-an-AW-meet-er). A sphygmomanometer works by putting pressure on the blood vessels in your arm to stop the flow of blood for a few seconds. As the pressure of the device is released, a doctor listens for the sound of normal blood flow as it returns. The difference in pressure between normal blood flow and reduced blood flow tells the doctor what the blood pressure is.

Anything that blocks blood vessels can cause problems for the whole system. For instance, arteries are blood vessels that carry blood away from the heart. Arteries carry blood under high pressure. If arteries become blocked, blood pressure can get too high or too low. If the arteries get hard, they can burst and blood will leak out.

Name

Date

Section

9.3

Summary

continued

How is the respiratory system like a pneumatic system?

The **respiratory system** is the body system that brings air into the body and removes carbon dioxide from the body. Breathing involves changes in air pressure inside and outside your body.

When you inhale, your chest expands because muscles between your ribs push the ribs apart to make a bigger space. Also, a sheet of muscle in the lower chest, called the **diaphragm**, moves downward to make a bigger space. The bigger space in your chest makes the air pressure inside your lungs lower. The air outside your body is higher in pressure. So the air rushes into your body and into your lungs. When you exhale, the air pressure inside your lungs gets higher. Air is pushed out of your lungs and out of your body. ✓

Anything that blocks the passages that carry air in and out of your body can cause problems for the whole system. Passages can swell up from infections. This makes them more narrow on the inside, so you have more trouble breathing. A disease called asthma also makes the passages narrower. People with asthma have great trouble breathing. They can use an inhaler, which brings medicine to the passages to reduce the swelling.

✓ *Reading Check*

2. How is the respiratory system like a pneumatic system?

_____

_____

_____

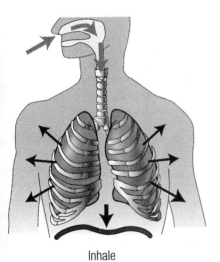

Inhale

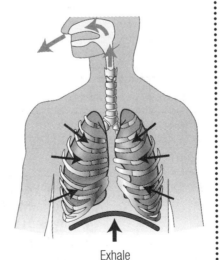

Exhale

Use with textbook pages 334–339.

Fluid systems puzzle

Across	Down
1. involves changes in air pressure inside and outside your body	2. system that brings air into the body
5. system that transports blood	3. liquid flowing in blood vessels
11. measures blood pressure	4. carry blood through the body
12. pressure can increase when arteries are _____	6. can cause passages to swell
	7. muscle in chest
13. increases and decreases between heartbeats	8. disease that makes it hard to breathe
	9. pumps blood around the body
	10. carry blood under high pressure

Name _____   Date _____

Use with textbook pages 334–339.

Pressure in the human body

Vocabulary	
blood	higher
blood pressure	inhale
blood vessels	lower
breathing	pressure
circulatory	pump
diaphragm	respiratory
exhale	sphygmomanometer
heart	

Use the terms in the vocabulary box to fill in the blanks. You can use each term as many times as necessary. You will not need to use all the terms.

1. The _____ system transports blood through the body.

2. The circulatory system is made up of the _____, blood vessels, and _____.

3. The heart is a _____ that keeps blood moving through blood vessels.

4. Blood must be kept under _____ so it can reach all parts of the body.

5. Blood pressure is measured with a _____.

6. Arteries are _____ that carry blood away from the heart. If arteries become blocked, _____ can get too high or too low.

7. The _____ system is the body system that brings air into the body and removes carbon dioxide from the body.

8. _____ involves changes in air pressure inside and outside your body.

9. When you _____, your chest expands because muscles between your ribs push the ribs apart. A sheet of muscle in the lower chest called the _____ moves downward to make a bigger space.

10. The bigger space in your chest makes the air pressure inside your lungs lower. The air outside your body is _____ in pressure. So the air rushes into your body and into your lungs.

Use with textbook pages 334–339.

A world of fluid systems

Create a colourful collage of the natural fluid systems that exist around us in the atmosphere, deep inside the Earth, and in the ocean. Cut out pictures and photographs of natural fluid systems from magazines and newspapers. Paste them in the box below. If you prefer, you could draw and colour examples instead. Label each example.

Use with textbook pages 334–339.

Natural fluid systems

Match the Term on the left with the best Descriptor on the right. Each Descriptor may be used only once.

Term	Descriptor
1. _____ diaphragm 2. _____ blood pressure 3. _____ circulatory system 4. _____ respiratory system 5. _____ sphygmomanometer	A. moves blood around the body B. a sheet of muscle that helps breathing C. measures blood pressure D. increases and decreases between heartbeats E. brings air into the body and removes carbon dioxide from blood F. carries blood under high pressure away for the heart

Circle the letter of the best answer.

6. Which of the following is not a part or an example of a natural fluid system?

   A. heart

   B. lungs

   C. hurricane

   D. car brakes

7. Which of the following is correct about the heart and lungs?

I.	the heart: part of a hydraulic system
II.	the lungs: part of a hydraulic system
III.	the heart: part of a pneumatic system
IV.	the lungs: part of a pneumatic system

   A. I and II

   B. I and IV

   C. II and III

   D. III and IV

8. Which of the following has a similar purpose to a pump in a hydraulic system?

   A. the heart

   B. the lungs

   C. the blood

   D. the diaphragm

9. What happens when your chest expands as you inhale?

   A. the volume of the lungs increases and the pressure inside rises

   B. the volume of the lungs decreases and the pressure inside rises

   C. the volume of the lung decreases and the pressure inside lowers

   D. the volume of the lungs increases and the pressure inside lowers

10. What happens when you exhale?

   A. the air pressure inside your lungs gets higher, so air is pushed out of your lungs

   B. the air pressure inside your lungs gets lower, so air is pushed out of your lungs

   C. the air pressure inside your lungs gets higher, so air is pulled into your lungs

   D. the air pressure inside your lungs gets lower, so air is pulled into your lungs

11. Which of the following describes what an asthma attack does to the pathway to the lungs?

   A. causes it to lengthen

   B. causes it to widen

   C. causes it to narrow

   D. causes it to fill up with fluid

Distribution of Water

Textbook pages 362–367

Before You Read

What is the source of the water that you use? How is more water added to the source? Write your thoughts on the lines below. Then read on to find out how changes of state make water available on Earth.

Mark the Text

Reinforce Your Understanding

As you read this section, highlight the main point of each sentence or paragraph. Use a different colour to highlight an example that helps explain the main point, or write your own.

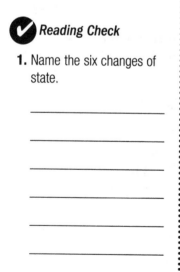

Reading Check

1. Name the six changes of state.

_____

_____

_____

_____

_____

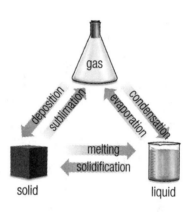

How does water change state?

Water, like other types of matter, can change state when is heated or cooled.

◆ Heating liquid water makes it evaporate. **Evaporation** is a change of state from a liquid to a gas.

◆ Cooling water vapour makes it condense. **Condensation** is a change of state from a gas to a liquid.

◆ Heating solid water (ice) makes it melt. **Melting** is a change of state from a solid to a liquid.

◆ Cooling liquid water makes it freeze (become a solid). **Solidification** is a change of state from a liquid to a solid. The **freezing point** is the temperature at which solidification takes place for any type of matter.

◆ Heating ice can also make it sublimate. **Sublimation** is the change of state from a solid directly into a gas.

◆ A gas changing directly to a solid is called **deposition**. ✔

Name

Date

Section

10.1

Summary

continued

What is the water cycle?

Water is a gas (water vapour) in the air. Water is a liquid in ponds, lakes, rivers, and oceans. Water is a solid in ice and snow.

The water cycle is the process by which water on Earth changes from state to state. This process takes place all the time. Water is always changing state from solid to liquid to gas to liquid to solid, over and over, in a constant cycle.

When it is heated by the Sun, some of the water in lakes and the ocean evaporates and becomes water vapour (gas). When the water vapour in the air cools, it falls to Earth as precipitation. The precipitation may be liquid (rain) or solid (snow or hail). Some of the precipitation falls on lakes, rivers, and the ocean. Then it evaporates again and the cycle continues.

Why is water important?

All forms of life on Earth need water to survive. Sometimes it can be hard to find enough fresh, clean water for everyone's needs. A **hydrologist** is a scientist who studies the water cycle to know how and where water is found on Earth. A hydrologist helps to make sure people always have fresh, clean water. ✔

Reading Check

2. What is a hydrologist?

_____

_____

_____

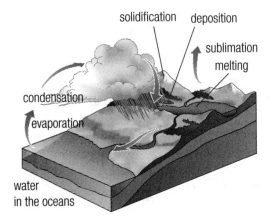

precipitation: water comes back to the ground as a liquid or a solid (rain or snow)

solidification   deposition

sublimation

melting

condensation

evaporation

water in the oceans

Use with textbook pages 362–365.

The water cycle

Vocabulary	
boiling point	melting
condensation	solid
deposition	solidification
evaporation	sublimation
freezing point	the Sun
hydrologist	water cycle
ice	water vapour
liquid	

Use the terms in the vocabulary box above to fill in the blanks. Use each term only once. You do not need to use all the terms.

1. Water in the air is called _____.
   Water is in the _____ state in lakes and ponds.
   Water in the solid state is _____.

2. The process by which water changes from state to state on Earth is called the
   _____.

3. The heat for the water cycle comes mainly from _____.

4. The change of state from liquid to gas is called _____.
   The change from liquid to solid is called _____.

5. The temperature at which solidification takes place is called the
   _____.

6. The change of state from a gas to a liquid is called _____.
   The change from a gas to a solid is called _____.

7. The change of state from a solid to a liquid is called _____.
   The change of state of a solid to a gas is called _____.

8. A _____ studies the water cycle to know how and where
   water is found on Earth.

Use with textbook page 364.

Changing state

Use the spaces below to explain whether heat is being added or released. Also, describe how the state of the water changes.

Term	Is heat added or released?	Change in state from _____ to _____
1. evaporation		_____ to _____
2. melting		_____ to _____
3. condensation		_____ to _____
4. solidification		_____ to _____
5. deposition		_____ to _____
6. sublimation		_____ to _____

Fill in the missing labels. Draw and label the two missing diagrams.

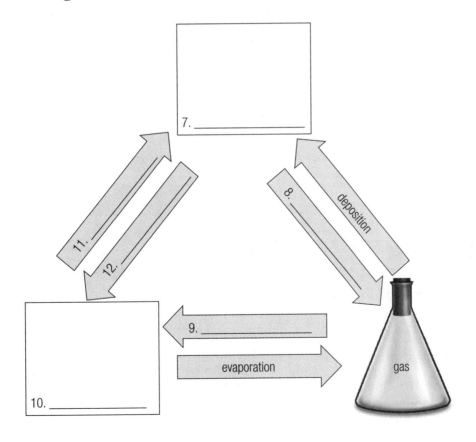

Use with textbook page 365.

The water cycle

The water cycle happens because heat energy is constantly being added or taken away from water in its various states. The driving force behind the water cycle is the Sun.

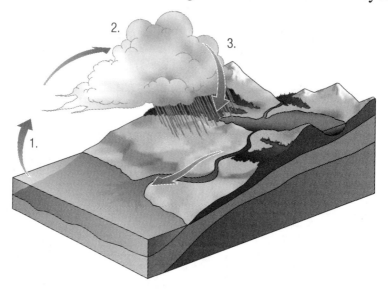

Explain what is happening during each stage of the water cycle.

1. _____

_____

_____

_____

_____

2. _____

_____

_____

_____

_____

3. _____

_____

_____

_____

_____

Use with textbook pages 362–367.

Distribution of water

Match the Term on the left with the best Descriptor on the right. Each Descriptor may be used only once.	
Term	**Descriptor**
1. _____ precipitation 2. _____ water cycle 3. _____ heat from the Sun	**A.** ground water **B.** causes evaporation **C.** water keeps on changing state **D.** rain, snow, sleet, and hail

Circle the letter of the best answer.

4. Evaporation occurs when

   A. gas changes to liquid

   B. gas changes to solid

   C. liquid changes to solid

   D. liquid changes to gas

5. Sublimation occurs when

   A. solid changes to gas

   B. gas changes to solid

   C. solid changes to liquid

   D. liquid changes to solid

6. Deposition occurs when

   A. liquid water becomes ice

   B. ice becomes water vapour

   C. liquid water becomes water vapour

   D. water vapour becomes ice

7. Condensation occurs when

   A. a liquid is cooled

   B. a gas is cooled

   C. a liquid is heated

   D. a gas is heated

8. Melting occurs when

   A. a solid is heated

   B. a liquid is heated

   C. a gas is heated

   D. all of the above

9. Solidification occurs when

   A. a liquid is cooled

   B. a gas is cooled

   C. a liquid is heated

   D. a gas is heated

10. A hydrologist studies

   A. the water cycle

   B. where water is found on Earth

   C. neither A nor B

   D. both A and B

11. Which statements are true of the water cycle?

I.	Water vapour changes to liquid water.
II.	Liquid water changes to ice.
III.	Ice melts to become liquid water.
IV.	Liquid water evaporates to become a gas.

   A. I, III, and IV only

   B. II and III only

   C. I and IV only

   D. I, II, III, and IV

How Ocean Water Differs from Fresh Water

Textbook pages 368–375

Before You Read

If you have ever tasted ocean water, you know that it is salty. Where did all the salt come from? Write your ideas on the lines below.

Identify the Main Idea
As you read this section, stop after every paragraph and put what you read into your own words. Highlight the main idea in each paragraph.

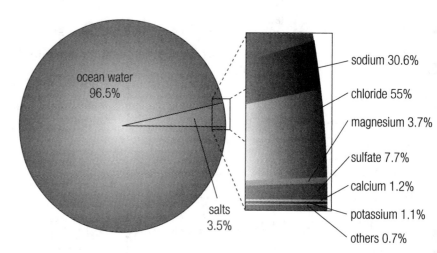

ocean water 96.5%

salts 3.5%

sodium 30.6%

chloride 55%

magnesium 3.7%

sulfate 7.7%

calcium 1.2%

potassium 1.1%

others 0.7%

Percentage by mass of dissolved solids in ocean water

Why is ocean water salty?

Most of the water that falls to the ground does not stay where it falls. Some of the water falls into streams and rivers. Some of the water flows on the surface and then joins streams and rivers. And some water seeps into the ground.

Many substances dissolve easily in water. Salt is one of these substances. As water moves over the ground and rocks, it picks up salt and other substances. Sooner or later, the moving water finds its way into the ocean. When it does, the salt and other substances that were carried by the water also enter the ocean. This process has been going on for millions of years.

Volcanoes on the ocean floor add salt and other substances directly into the water. Volcanoes on land send out substances high into the air. Some of this matter falls right into the ocean. Some of it falls to Earth's surface and is carried to the ocean by water as the water flows over the ground. ●

1. Where does the salt in ocean water come from?

_____

_____

_____

What is salinity?

The amount of salt that is dissolved in water is called
salinity. Ocean water has a lot of salt in it, so ocean water
has a high salinity. River water has much less salt in it than
ocean water does, so river water has a much lower salinity.

There are many kinds of salt that add to the salinity of the
ocean. One kind is called sodium chloride. It is the same kind
of salt that we add to food. About 85 percent of the salt in the
ocean is sodium chloride.

Do all parts of the ocean have the same salinity?

◆ Ocean water is saltier near the North and South Poles
  because when the water freezes, it leaves salt behind.

◆ Ocean water is very salty near the equator because when
  water evaporates it leaves the salt behind.

◆ Ocean water near continents is less salty than in the
  middle of the ocean because fresh water from rivers
  dilutes the ocean water.

Does ocean water have the same density as fresh water?

Density is the amount of mass in a given volume of a
material. Ocean water has a higher density than fresh water
because ocean water has more salt in it. If you measured the
mass of 1 L of ocean water and 1 L of fresh water, what do
you think you would find? For these same volumes, the mass
of the ocean water would be greater than the mass of the
fresh water. In other words, the density of the ocean water
would be greater.

Ocean water has a lower freezing point than fresh water.
This means that ocean water freezes (becomes solid) at a
lower temperature than fresh water does. ✓

✔ Reading Check

2. Why is ocean water more
dense than fresh water?

_____

_____

_____

Use with textbook pages 368–371.

Ocean water

Vocabulary	
density	more
dissolve	North and South Poles
equator	ocean floor
greater	salinity
land	sodium chloride
less	volume
mass	

Use the terms in the vocabulary box to fill in the blanks. Use each term only once. You do not need to use all the terms.

1. Many substances, such as salt, _____ easily in water.

2. Volcanoes on the _____ add salt and other substances right into the water.

3. Volcanoes on _____ send out substances high into the air.

4. The amount of salt that is dissolved in water is called _____.

5. Ocean water is saltier near the _____ because when the water freezes, it leaves salt behind.

6. Ocean water is very salty near the _____ because when water evaporates it leaves the salt behind.

7. Ocean water near continents is _____ salty than in the middle of the ocean because fresh water from rivers dilutes the ocean water.

8. More than 85 percent of the salt in the ocean is made from _____.

9. The amount of mass in a given volume of a material is called _____.

10. Ocean water has a _____ density than fresh water because ocean water has more salt in it.

e with textbook pages 368–371.

alt water

nswer the questions in the spaces provided.

l. What happens to the water that falls to the ground?

_____

_____

_____

_____

?. How does the water on land add salt to the ocean?

_____

_____

_____

l. How do volcanoes add salt to the oceans?

_____

_____

_____

l. Why are some parts of the ocean saltier than other parts?

_____

_____

_____

_____

l. What is density?

_____

_____

_____

l. Which is denser, ocean water or fresh water?

_____

'. Which has a higher freezing point, ocean water or fresh water?

_____

Use with textbook pages 368–371.

Dissolved solids

**List the dissolved solids in water in order from the smallest percentage to the
largest percentage.**

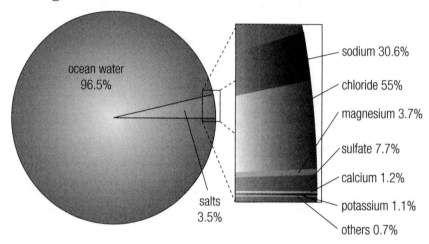

ocean water
96.5%

salts
3.5%

sodium 30.6%

chloride 55%

magnesium 3.7%

sulfate 7.7%

calcium 1.2%

potassium 1.1%

others 0.7%

Percentage by mass of dissolved solids
in ocean water

1. _____   **smallest percentage**

2. _____

3. _____

4. _____

5. _____

6. _____

7. _____   **largest percentage**

8. What percentage of the total mass of dissolved solids is sodium chloride? Show you
work below.

_____

9. What percentage of the total mass are dissolved solids other than sodium chloride?
Show your work below.

_____

se with textbook pages 368–371.

low ocean water differs rom fresh water

Match the Term on the left with the best Descriptor on the right. Each Descriptor may be used only once.

Term	Descriptor
1. _____ density 2. _____ salinity	**A.** amount of water dissolved in salt **B.** amount of salt dissolved in water **C.** amount of mass in a given volume of material **D.** amount of volume in a given mass of material

ircle the letter of the best answer.

3. Where do dissolved solids in the ocean come from?

I.	water on the ground
II.	volcanoes on the ocean floor
III.	volcanoes on land

A. I and II only

B. I and III only

C. II and III only

D. I, II, and III

4. Which of these statements is true?

A. Salinity is the same everywhere in the ocean.

B. Salinity is higher near the equator and the North and South Poles

C. Salinity is higher near the continents.

D. Salinity is higher where rivers enter the ocean.

5. How do the freezing points of ocean water and fresh water compare?

A. they are the same

B. ocean water has a lower freezing point

C. fresh water has a lower freezing point

D. ocean water does not freeze

6. How does the salinity of ocean water and fresh water compare?

A. ocean water has a higher salinity

B. fresh water has a higher salinity

C. they are the same

D. fresh water has no salinity

7. How does the density of ocean water and fresh water compare?

A. ocean water has a higher density

B. fresh water has a higher density

C. they are the same

8. How does the mass of 1 L of ocean water and 1 L of fresh water compare?

A. ocean water has a greater mass

B. fresh water has a greater mass

C. they are the same

9. What percentage of the salt in the ocean is sodium chloride?

A. 30.6%

B. 55%

C. 85.6%

D. 100%

Sources of Fresh Water

Textbook pages 376–385

Before You Read

Do people in cities, towns, and on farms all use the same sources for their water? Record your thoughts on the lines below.

_____

_____

 **Mark the Text**

Summarize
As you read this section, highlight the main point or points in each paragraph. Then write a short paragraph summarizing what you have learned.

What are the sources of fresh water on Earth?

The water that people use to drink and wash comes from rain and snow that runs off the land. The run-off water flows into lakes, streams, and rivers. It also seeps into the ground and collects below Earth's surface.

What is run-off?

Water runs off the land because gravity acts on it. **Gravity** is a force that pulls all things toward the centre of Earth. Because of gravity, things that are higher naturally move toward a point that is lower. Water runs off along Earth's surface because gravity pulls it from places that are higher to places that are lower.

A drainage basin is an area of land that drains run-off into a body of water such as a stream, a river, or a lake. Many people use fresh water that comes from lakes and rivers. Other living things depend on this water, too.

How do we use water that seeps into the ground?

Most of the rain that falls on land seeps out of sight into the ground. Below the surface, this water trickles downward through pores (spaces) and cracks in the rock. Water that moves into and through pores and cracks of underground rock is called **ground water**.

Ground water is an important source of water for many people. They drill wells into the ground to draw water up so it can be used. ✓

✓ **Reading Check**

1. Where does ground water come from?

_____

_____

_____

How do glaciers affect the water cycle?

Most of the fresh water on Earth is frozen. People cannot use much of this water, because it is trapped as ice. **Glaciers** are huge masses of snow and ice that move. There are two types of glaciers:

◆ Alpine glaciers (also called valley glaciers) form in mountains. They move slowly downhill through mountain ranges.

◆ Continental glaciers are much bigger than alpine glaciers. They cover large areas of land and are often called ice sheets. Continental glaciers are found in the Arctic and in the Antarctic.

Glaciers affect the water cycle by "holding" water as ice. Less water evaporates from glaciers than from liquid bodies of water. ✔

Do glaciers ever melt?

The water in a glacier can stop moving downhill and can melt when the slow-moving glacier reaches a large body of water such as an ocean. As the front of the glacier slowly spills over the edge of the land, deep cracks called **crevasses** form. Large chunks of the glacier break off as gravity pulls down on them. When these large chunks of ice fall into the ocean, they are called **icebergs**.

The water in a glacier can stop moving downhill and can melt when the temperature is warm enough to melt the ice faster than the glacier can be moved forward by gravity. If temperatures increase, the glacier can start receding, which means it melts back up the slope. All glaciers in British Columbia and in most parts of the world are now receding.

✔ **Reading Check**

2. Why is the fresh water in a glacier unavailable for use by people?

_____

_____

_____

Use with textbook pages 376–381.

Fresh water

Vocabulary	
alpine	ground
continental	ground water
crevasses	icebergs
drainage basin	moving
frozen	receding
glaciers	run-off
gravity	wells

**Use the terms in the vocabulary box to fill in the blanks. Use each term only once.
You do not need to use all the terms.**

1. The water that people use to drink and wash comes from rain and snow that runs off
   the land. The _____ water flows into lakes, streams, and rivers.
   It also seeps into the _____ and collects below Earth's surface.

2. Water runs off along Earth's surface because _____ pulls it
   from places that are higher to places that are lower.

3. A _____ is an area of land that drains run-off into a body
   of water such as a stream, a river, or a lake.

4. Water that moves into and through pores and cracks of underground rock is called
   _____. People drill _____ into the
   ground to draw water up so it can be used.

5. _____ are huge masses of snow and ice that move.

6. _____ glaciers form in mountains.
   They move slowly downhill through mountain ranges.

7. _____ glaciers cover large areas of land
   and are often called ice sheets.

8. As the front of the glacier slowly spills over the edge of the land, deep cracks called
   _____ form. Large chunks of the glacier break off as gravity
   pulls down on them. When these large chunks of ice fall into the ocean, they are
   called _____.

9. If temperatures increase, the glacier can start _____,
   which means it melts back up the slope.

e with textbook pages 376–385.

rom sky to sea

reate your own six-part comic book story about a drop of water that falls as rain
nd eventually travels into the ocean. Use the terms you have learned in this section.
nclude both words and pictures to tell your story.

1.	2.	3.

4.	5.	6.

Use with textbook pages 376–385.

True or false?

Read the statements given below. If the statement is true, write "T" on the line in front of the statement. If it is false, write "F" and then rewrite the statement so it is true.

1. ____ Water runs along Earth's surface because gravity pulls it from lower places to higher places.

   _____

   _____

2. ____ A drainage basin drains ground water into a stream, river, or lake.

   _____

   _____

3. ____ Water that moves into and through pores and cracks or underground rock is called run-off.

   _____

   _____

4. ____ Most of the fresh water on Earth is in the ocean.

   _____

   _____

5. ____ Glaciers are only found in the Arctic and the Antarctic.

   _____

   _____

6. ____ Crevasses are large chunks of ice.

   _____

   _____

7. ____ If the temperature increases, a glacier can recede.

   _____

   _____

se with textbook pages 376–385.

ources of fresh water

Match the Term on the left with the best Descriptor on the right. Each Descriptor may be used only once.

Term	Descriptor
1. _____ crevasses	**A.** runs off
2. _____ glaciers	**B.** seeps downward
3. _____ gravity	**C.** deep cracks
4. _____ ground water	**D.** large chunks
	E. pulls downhill
5. _____ icebergs	**F.** huge masses

ircle the letter of the best answer.

6. Most of the fresh water on Earth is found in

   A. rain

   B. lakes

   C. rivers

   D. ice

7. Which of the following are sources of fresh water?

I.	ground water
II.	run-off water
III.	glaciers
IV.	ice

   A. I and II only

   B. I, II, and IV only

   C. II only

   D. I, II, III, and IV

8. Which statements about glaciers are true?

I.	Alpine glaciers are smaller than continental glaciers.
II.	Crevasses form as the glacier spills over the edge of the land.
III.	Icebergs are large chunks of ice that gravity pulls down to the ground.
IV.	Glaciers can only move downhill.

   A. I and II only

   B. I, II, and IV only

   C. II only

   D. I, II, III, and IV

9. A drainage basin

   A. drains run-off into a stream, river, or lake

   B. drains run-off into the ocean

   C. drains run-off into the ground

   D. does none of the above

10. All the glaciers now in British Columbia are

   A. receding

   B. slowly increasing

   C. increasing rapidly

   D. not changing at all

11. Where does ground water come from?

   A. wells

   B. drainage basins

   C. rain that seeps into the ground

   D. oceans

Water's Effect on Shaping Earth's Surface

Textbook pages 386–397

Before You Read

Water can shape Earth's surface in many ways. What examples can you think of? Write your thoughts on the lines below.

_____

_____

 *Mark the Text*

Create a Chart
Highlight the text that describes how water breaks down Earth's surface. In a different colour, highlight the text that describes how water builds up Earth's surface. Use the highlighted text to make a chart that shows how water shapes Earth's surface.

 *Reading Check*

1. What are the three main ways that water shapes Earth's surface?

_____

_____

_____

What role does water play in shaping Earth's surface?

Water breaks down Earth's surface in some places and builds it up in other places. Three main processes are involved.

1. **Weathering** causes changes that break down rocks into smaller and smaller pieces.

♦ The changes are called **physical weathering** if the rock that breaks down stays the same type of rock.

♦ The changes are called **chemical weathering** if the rock that breaks down becomes a different substance.

♦ If the physical or chemical weathering is caused by living things, it is then called **biological weathering**.

2. **Erosion** moves large and small rock pieces from one place to another.

3. **Deposition** drops or leaves rock pieces that have been carried by water from one place to another. ✔

Weathering and erosion act to break down Earth's surface. Deposition acts to build it up.

How do water and ice weather rock?

♦ Physical weathering: Water can collect in cracks and pores of rock. When the water freezes, it expands. This type of physical weathering can break the rock into smaller pieces.

◆ Chemical weathering: Rainwater is slightly acidic. As rain falls from the sky, it picks up pollutants that can make it more acidic. When it reaches the ground, the acidic rainwater dissolves some substances from rock on Earth's surface. The rock gets weaker and wears down or breaks into smaller pieces.

Acidic rainwater weathers rock under the ground, too. The acidic water dissolves rock that has calcium carbonate in it. As time passes, bigger and bigger gaps form large hollows in the rock, and can form an underground **cave**.

If the gaps caused by the water are near the surface, the ground at the surface may collapse. This causes a sinkhole to form. An area of land that has lots of sinkholes is called a **karst**.

How do water and ice erode rock?

As water moves over Earth's surface, the water can push rocks from one place to another. This happens especially in **rapids**, which are places of fast-moving water in a steep, rocky river. The tiny bits of rock that result from constant erosion by water become sediments.

When rain soaks the sides of steep hills and mountains, the force of gravity can cause part of the slope to fall away as a **landslide**.

As glaciers move over Earth's surface, the ice acts like sandpaper. It picks up and carries away rock material. It also scrapes the ground beneath it. The scratch marks that are visible when the ice melts are called **striations**.

How do water and ice deposit rock?

When moving water slows down and when moving ice melts, the rocks they carry are released. These deposits build up as time passes. When this happens in the place where a river enters a lake or ocean, the deposits form a fan-shape called a **delta**.

✔ *Reading Check*

2. What are three examples of how water and ice erode rock?

_____

_____

_____

Use with textbook pages 386–395.

Shaping Earth's surface

Vocabulary	
acidic	glacier
biological	karst
calcium carbonate	landslide
cave	physical
chemical	rapids
deposition	sinkhole
erosion	striations

Use the terms in the vocabulary box to fill in the blanks. Use each term only once. You do not need to use all the terms.

1. Weathering is called _____ if the rock that breaks down stays the same type of rock. Weathering is called _____ if the rock that breaks down becomes a different substance. If the weathering is caused by living things, it is then called _____.

2. _____ moves large and small rock pieces from one place to another. _____ drops or leaves rock pieces that have been carried by water from one place to another.

3. Rainwater is slightly _____. When it reaches the ground, the acidic rainwater dissolves some substances from rock on Earth's surface.

4. Acidic water dissolves rock that has _____ in it. As time passes, bigger and bigger gaps form large hollows in the rock, and we call this a _____.

5. If the gaps caused by the water form near the surface, the ground at the surface may collapse. This causes a _____ to form. An area of land that has lots of sinkholes is called a _____.

6. As water moves over Earth's surface, it can push rocks from one place to another. This happens especially in _____, which are places of fast-moving water in a steep, rocky river.

7. As glaciers move over Earth's surface, the ice acts like sandpaper. The scratch marks that are visible when the ice melts are called _____

Name _____ Date _____

Comprehension

Section 10.4

Use with textbook pages 386–395.

The effect of water

Answer the questions below.

1. What are the three main processes by which water breaks down the Earth's landscape?

_____

2. What does weathering do?

_____

_____

3. What is an example of physical weathering?

_____

4. What is an example of chemical weathering?

_____

5. How is erosion different from weathering?

_____

_____

6. How does a cave form?

_____

_____

7. How does a karst form?

_____

_____

8. How does water erode rocks in rivers?

_____

_____

9. How does water erode rock on steep hills?

_____

10. How is a delta formed?

_____

Use with textbook pages 386–395.

Earth's surface puzzle

Complete the following crossword puzzle.

Across
4. a large underground hollow in rock
6. scratch marks cut into rock by glaciers moving over it
7. the movement of rock pieces from one place to another
9. rainfall that can dissolve calcium carbonate
11. the process in which eroded rocks are dropped off
12. weathering caused by living things

Down
1. weathering in which rock stays the same type of rock
2. an area of many sinkholes
3. the gradual process of breaking down rock into smaller pieces
5. a sudden, rapid movement of rock material down the slope of a hill or mountain
8. an area of fast moving, churning water in a steep, rocky river
10. fan-shaped area of rock deposits
13. weathering in which rock is changed into another type of rock

se with textbook pages 386–395

Water's effect on shaping Earth's surface

Match the Term on the left with the best Descriptor on the right. Each Descriptor may only be used once.	
Term	**Descriptor**
1. _____ cave 2. _____ delta 3. _____ deposition 4. _____ erosion 5. _____ karst 6. _____ landslide 7. _____ rapids 8. _____ striations 9. _____ weathering	**A.** a large underground hollow in rock **B.** scratch marks cut into rock by glaciers **C.** the movement of rock pieces from one place to another **D.** the process in which eroded rocks are dropped off **E.** an area of many sinkholes **F.** the gradual process of breaking down rock into smaller pieces **G.** a sudden, rapid movement of rock material down a slope **H.** an area of fast moving water in a steep, rocky river **I.** fan-shaped area of rock deposits **J.** weathering in which rock is changed into another substance

Circle the letter of the best answer.

10. Which of the following is an example of physical weathering?

A. acidic rainwater falls on rocks

B. water freezes in cracks in rocks

C. rocks are deposited in a delta

D. caves form underground

11. Which of the following are examples of chemical weathering?

I.	karst
II.	cave
III.	sinkhole

A. I and II only

B. II and III only

C. I and III only

D. I, II, and III

12. Water shapes Earth's surface through

A. erosion

B. deposition

C. weathering

D. all of the above

13. How does ice weather rock?

I.	ice in small cracks in the rock breaks the rock
II.	ice in glaciers acts like sandpaper as it moves over rocks
III.	ice dissolves rock
IV.	ice pushes rocks against each other in rapids

A. I and II only

B. III and IV only

C. I, III, and IV only

D. II, III, and IV only

Ocean Basins

Textbook pages 402–413

Before You Read

If you could take all the water out of the ocean, what would you see? Write your thoughts on the lines below or make a sketch.

_____

_____

 **Mark the Text**

Identify Definitions
Highlight the definition of each word that appears in bold type. Make a chart or sketch to help you understand what each word means.

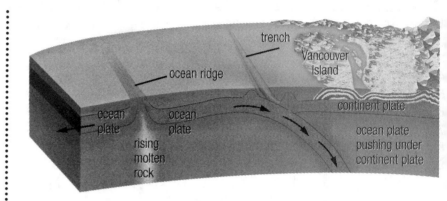

 **Reading Check**

1. What are tectonic processes?

_____

_____

_____

What is the bottom of the ocean like?

The bottom of the ocean has features like those you would see on land. There are ranges of mountains. There are steep, deep valleys. There are vast, flat plains.

These features are different from those on land in two main ways. First, the features are much larger. Second, the forces that shape these features are different from the forces that shape landforms. There are no winds, rivers, rain, or ice at the bottom of the ocean to erode rock. Instead, the main force that shapes the ocean basins is the movement of Earth's crust.

How does the movement of Earth's crust shape the ocean basins?

Earth's crust is made up of huge sections of rock called tectonic plates. These plates float on a layer of molten (melted) rock. Some plates lie under the bottom of the ocean. Others lie under the continents. The movement of the plates and the way they interact are called **tectonic processes.**

In the middle of the ocean, the ocean plates move apart as molten rock pushes up from underneath them. As the molten rock pushes up into the ocean water, the rock cools and becomes solid. This process creates huge mountain systems called mid-ocean ridges.

Closer to land, ocean plates move under continent plates. This process creates deep ocean valleys, called trenches, at the base of some continents. ✅

What are the features of an ocean basin?

The shallowest part of the continental margin that runs out into the ocean from the shoreline is called the **continental shelf**. The shelf slopes gradually away from the shore for tens or hundreds of kilometres. Then it drops steeply downward. From the point at which this steep drop occurs to the ocean basin is the **continental slope**.

At the base of the slope is a more gentle slope called the **continental rise**. It is made of sediments carried by **turbidity currents**, which are underwater landslides from the continental slope. Some powerful turbidity currents scrape out large parts of the continental shelf and slope to form deep gullies called **submarine canyons**. ✅

The broad, flat region in the middle of the ocean basin is called the **abyssal plain**. The abyssal plain is surrounded by the rising outer edges of the **continental margin**.

✅ *Reading Check*

2. What features are part of the continental margin?

_____

_____

_____

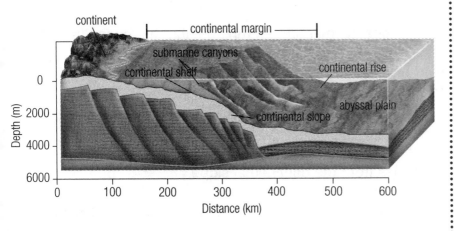

Use with textbook pages 404–409.

The ocean floor

Vocabulary	
abyssal plain	molten rock
continental margin	submarine canyons
continental shelf	tectonic plates
continental slope	tectonic processes
continental rise	trenches
landforms	turbidity currents
mid-ocean ridges	

Use the terms in the vocabulary box to fill in the blanks. Each term may be used as often as needed. You will not need to use all the terms.

1. Earth's crust is made up of huge sections of rock called _____ that float on a layer of _____.

2. The movement of the plates and the way they interact are called _____.

3. In the middle of the ocean, the ocean plates move apart as _____ pushes up from underneath them. As it pushes up into the ocean water, it cools and becomes solid. This process creates huge mountain systems called _____.

4. Closer to land, ocean plates move under continent plates. This process creates deep ocean valleys called _____ at the base of some continents.

5. The shallowest part of the continental margin that runs out into the ocean from the shoreline is called the _____. It slopes gradually, then it drops steeply downward. From the point at which this steep drop occurs to the ocean basin is the _____.

6. At the base of the slope is the _____. It is made of sediments carried by _____, which are underwater landslides from the continental slope.

7. Some powerful turbidity currents scrape out large parts of the continental shelf and slope to form deep gullies called _____.

8. The middle part of the ocean bottom is the ocean basin. This broad, flat region is called the _____. It is surrounded by the rising outer edges of the _____.

Use with textbook pages 406–409.

Features of the ocean floor

Examine the pictures below. Answer the questions.

A.

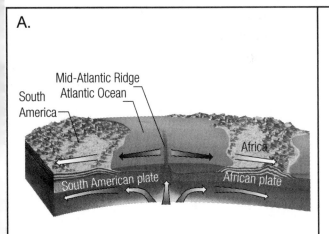

1. What events cause the formation of mid-ocean ridges?

B.

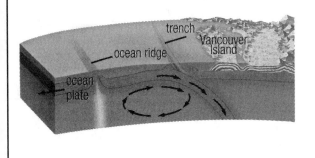

2. What events cause the formation of ocean trenches?

C.

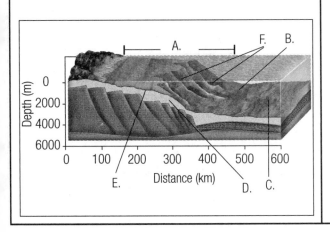

3. Name the features:

A.

B.

C.

D.

E.

F.

Use with textbook pages 400–409.

On the bottom of the ocean

Imagine that you are the pilot of small undersea exploration vehicle. You are exploring the ocean bottom. You travel from the shore (Box 1) out to the middle of the ocean (Box 4). Use words and pictures to describe your journey. Remember to use the proper terms for all the features that you see.

Box 1

Box 2

Box 3

Box 4

Use textbook pages 402–413.

Ocean basins

Match the Term on the left with the best Descriptor on the right. Each Descriptor may be used only once.	
Term	**Descriptor**
1. _____ abyssal plain	**A.** underwater mountains
2. _____ continental shelf	**B.** movement of the plates
3. _____ continental slope	**C.** steep drop in the continental margin
4. _____ continental rise	**D.** deep gullies
5. _____ submarine canyon	**E.** shallowest part of the continental margin
6. _____ tectonic processes	**F.** gentle slope in the continental margin
7. _____ turbidity current	**G.** broad, flat region in the middle of the ocean
	H. underwater landslide

Circle the letter of the best answer.

8. The continental margin

   A. is the plate under a continent

   B. is part of the continental shelf

   C. extends from a continent to the abyssal plain

   D. is the shoreline of a continent

9. The main force that shapes the ocean bottom is the movement of

   A. Earth's crust

   B. the continents

   C. turbidity currents

   D. underwater landslides

10. Trenches are formed when

   A. ocean plates move under continent plates

   B. continent plates move under ocean plates

   C. continent plates and ocean plates move apart

   D. none of the above

11. Ocean plates move apart when

   A. turbidity currents push them apart

   B. molten rock pushes up

   C. trenches are formed

   D. all of the above

12. Which features can be found on both the ocean floor and on continents?

   A. mid-ocean ridges, mountains, and valleys

   B. mountains, valleys, and plains

   C. turbidity currents, valleys, and plains

   D. none of the above

13. Mid-ocean ridges are formed when

   A. ocean plates move apart

   B. ocean plates move under continent plates

   C. continent plates move under ocean plates

   D. turbidity currents happen

14. Which of the following is not a feature of the ocean bottom?

   A. continental shelf

   B. continental slope

   C. continental floor

   D. continental rise

Ocean Currents

Textbook pages 414–427

Before You Read

What forces do you think cause ocean water to move? Do you think ocean water moves the same way everywhere in the ocean? Write your thoughts on the lines below.

_____

_____

 *Mark the Text*

Summarize

As you read this section, highlight the main point in each sentence or paragraph. Then use point form or a short paragraph to summarize what you have learned.

What is an ocean current?

Ocean water is always moving. One type of movement is a current. An **ocean current** is a large mass of ocean water that moves in a single direction through the ocean. There are two types of ocean currents: surface currents and deep water currents.

Type of ocean current	Causes	Effects in the ocean
surface current: a current that flows in the top 200 m of the ocean	1. **wind action**: the force of the wind blowing over the top of the water 2. spin of Earth 3. shape of the continents	• The speed and path of the surface currents is linked to the speed and path of the wind as it moves over the water. • As wind and water flow over Earth's surface, Earth spins under them from west to east. This pushes currents in the northern hemisphere to the right (toward the east). In the southern hemisphere, currents are pushed to the left (toward the west). • When moving water meets a solid land surface, the water is forced to flow in a different direction.
deep water current: a current that flows deeper than 200 m, as far as the bottom of the ocean	1. temperature of the water at different depths 2. salinity (saltiness) of ocean water	• Colder water is more dense, so it sinks and flows along the ocean bottom. Saltier water is also more dense, so it also sinks. • The nutrient-rich cold water is pushed to the ocean's surface by even colder, denser water moving in behind. This movement of cool water to the surface is an upwelling. The nutrients are food for **plankton**, which are microscopic plants and animals. In turn, the plankton are food for fish. ✓

✔ *Reading Check*

1. How is a surface current different from a deep water current?

_____

_____

_____

How else does ocean water move?

Water moves in waves across the ocean surface. Large, rolling waves that form out in the open ocean are called **swells**. Swells are caused mainly by winds. The biggest and strongest waves are made by tectonic forces. A huge, powerful wave that results from an underwater earthquake is called a **tsunami**.

Waves that reach the shore change the shape of the land. They can erode (carve away) rocky coastlines. They can also carry and deposit sediments to form beaches.

How do tides make water move?

Ocean water rises and falls in a regular cycle called **tides**. Tides are caused by the force of gravity of the Moon and the Sun pulling on our planet. The water on the side of Earth facing the Moon is pulled toward the Moon. This causes a bulge—a rise in the water level. This is a high tide. There is also a high tide on the side of Earth facing away from the Moon. The water between the two high tides is pulled toward the bulges. This causes the water level to fall in those regions. These are called low tides. ✓

When the Sun and the Moon are in line, high tides are even higher and low tides are even lower. These tides, called spring tides, happen because the Sun adds its strong force of gravity to the Moon's. When the Sun and Moon are at right angles to each other relative to Earth, the effect of gravity is less. With these tides, called neap tides, high tides are not as high and low tides are not as low.

✔ **Reading Check**

2. How do tides make water move?

_____

_____

_____

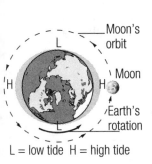

L = low tide H = high tide

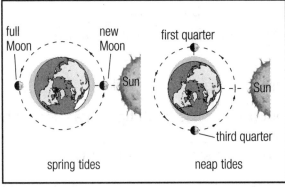

(not to scale)

Use with textbook pages 414–424.

Currents and waves

Vocabulary	
deep ocean current	surface current
density	swells
gravity	tectonic forces
high tide	temperature
low tides	tides
neap tides	tsunami
ocean current	upwelling
plankton	water level
salinity	winds
spring tides	wind action

Use the terms in the vocabulary box to fill in the blanks. You can use each term as many times as needed. You will not need to use all the terms.

1. A(n) _____ is a large mass of ocean water that moves in a single direction through the ocean. There are two types of ocean currents: _____ and _____.

2. The force of the wind blowing over the top of the water is called _____.

3. The two causes of deep ocean currents are the _____ of the water at different depths and the _____ of ocean water. Both causes lead to differences in _____.

4. The movement of cool water to the surface is a(n) _____.

5. Microscopic plants and animals are called _____.

6. Large, rolling waves that form out in the open ocean are called _____.

7. The biggest and strongest waves are made by _____. A huge, powerful wave that results from an underwater earthquake is called a(n) _____.

8. Ocean water rises and falls in a regular cycle called _____.

9. When the Sun and the Moon are in line, high tides are even higher and low tides are even lower. These tides, called _____, happen because the Sun adds its strong force of gravity to the Moon's.

10. When the Sun and Moon are at right angles to each other, the effect of gravity is less. With these tides, called _____, high tides are not as high and low tides are not as low.

Use with textbook pages 414–424.

True or false?

Read the statements given below. If the statement is true, write "T" on the line in front of the sentence. If it is false, write "F." Then rewrite the sentence to make it true.

1. _____ An ocean current is a large amount of ocean water that moves in many directions.

_____

_____

2. _____ Surface currents are caused by wind action, the spin of Earth, and temperature differences.

_____

_____

3. _____ Deep ocean currents are caused by salinity differences and the shape of the continents.

_____

_____

4. _____ Density differences draw warm water from deep in the ocean to the surface.

_____

_____

5. _____ The movement of warm water to the surface of the ocean is called an upwelling.

_____

_____

6. _____ Tides are caused by the force of gravity of the Moon and the Sun.

_____

_____

7. _____ Plankton are microscopic fish.

_____

8. _____ Waves that reach the shore change the shape of the land.

_____

_____

Use with textbook pages 423–424.

The ocean in motion

Draw diagrams to illustrate how the Sun, the Moon, and Earth affect the ocean. Label your diagrams.

1. Draw a diagram that shows how the Sun, the Moon, and Earth interact to form spring tides.

2. Draw a diagram that shows how the Sun, the Moon, and Earth interact to form neap tides.

Use with textbook pages 414–424.

Ocean currents

Match each Term on the left with the best Descriptor on the right. Each Descriptor may be used only once.

Term	Descriptor
1. _____ ocean current	A. large rolling ocean waves
2. _____ plankton	B. a large amount of ocean water that moves in a particular direction
3. _____ swells	C. a great ocean wave created by an underwater earthquake
4. _____ tides	D. microscopic plants and animals
5. _____ tsunami	E. the daily cycle of the rise and fall of ocean water
6. _____ wind action	F. due to differences in density
	G. causes the movement of surface currents

Circle the letter of the best answer.

7. Swells are caused mainly by

 A. tsunamis

 B. deep ocean currents

 C. surface currents

 D. wind

8. Tides are caused by

 A. the force of gravity of the Sun

 B. the force of gravity of the Moon

 C. both of the above

 D. neither of the above

9. Spring tides form when

 A. the Sun and the Moon are in line with Earth

 B. the Sun and the Moon are at right angles to each other

 C. both of the above

 D. neither of the above

10. Neap tides form when

 A. the Sun and the Moon are in line with Earth

 B. the Sun and the Moon are at right angles to each other

 C. both of the above

 D. neither of the above

11. Which of the following is true of ocean waves?

I.	they change the shape of the land
II.	they erode rocky coastlines
III.	they carry sediments
IV.	they deposit sediments to form beaches

 A. I and II only

 B. I and III only

 C. I, II, and IV only

 D. I, II, III, and IV

12. The biggest and strongest waves are made by

 A. wind

 B. gravity

 C. tectonic forces

 D. Earth's spin

Oceans and Climate

Textbook pages 428–435

Before You Read

Water plays a major role in moving heat all over Earth. How do you think that happens? Write your thoughts on the lines below.

_____

_____

Mark the Text

Identify Concepts
Highlight each question head in this section. Then use a different colour to highlight the answers to the questions.

Reading Check

1. What is the difference between weather and climate?

    _____

    _____

    _____

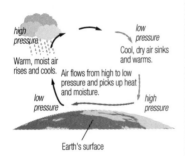

high pressure

low pressure
Cool, dry air sinks and warms.

Warm, moist air rises and cools. Air flows from high to low pressure and picks up heat and moisture.

low pressure

high pressure

Earth's surface

How is climate related to weather?

Weather is the state of the atmosphere at a given time. Weather includes features such as temperature, wind, air pressure, and moisture. **Climate** is all the features of the weather for a certain region averaged over a long time. ✔

How can oceans affect weather and climate?

The Sun's heat is most intense at the equator. The Sun's heat becomes less intense as you go farther north and south to the Poles. Warm ocean currents start near the equator. These currents affect weather and climate by giving off their heat to the air. Water has a high **heat capacity**, which means that it takes a long time to heat up and to cool down. The high heat capacity of water means that ocean water can store a great deal of heat. Oceans move this heat all around the world.

One way that warm ocean water affects weather and climate is by transferring its heat to the air above the ocean surface. This happens mainly by a process called convection. **Convection** transfers heat by the flow of heated fluid.

Transfer of heat by wind is an example of convection. The wind that forms over water at the equator carries heat and moisture north and south toward each of the Poles. At the same time, the wind drives warm surface currents toward the Poles. This movement of air and water helps create Earth's weather systems.

How do warm and cool currents affect land?

The Gulf Stream is a warm current that flows north from the equator and along the east coast of North America to Canada. There it meets a cold current of water from the Arctic. This pushes the warm current east toward the British Isles and northern Europe. The warm current helps to keep the British Isles and northern Europe warmer in the winter and cooler in the summer. Meanwhile, the cold current from the Arctic brings colder, drier air to other northern places such as Labrador and Sweden.

In a similar way, warm currents off the coast of British Columbia bring warm, moist air to the coast. The mountains on the coast prevent this warm, moist air from reaching the interior of British Columbia. The interior tends to have cold, snowy winters and hot, dry summers.

What is el Niño and what does it do?

Normally, the winds in the Pacific Ocean blow warm currents west along the equator. This creates very warm surface water temperatures in the western Pacific Ocean and upwelling in the eastern Pacific Ocean. Every few years, a change in this pattern happens. The Pacific winds are weaker and the warm water current starts to move east toward South America.

This event changes the patterns of wind and water currents. Wind currents are pushed off their common paths, so they deliver their heat and weather to different areas than usual. Places that usually get wet and cold weather get dry and warm weather. Places that usually have lots of rain get little or no rain. This change in the usual pattern of wind and water currents that produces unusual weather all over the world is called **el Niño**.

What is la Niña and what does it do?

An event that is like the reverse of el Niño is la Niña. **La Niña** is a period during which upwelling causes unusually cold water to rise to the surface off the coast of South America near the equator. It tends to bring wetter weather to places that are usually dry. ✔

Reading Check

2. What is the difference between el Niño and la Niña?

_____

_____

_____

Use textbook pages 430–431.

Convection and climate

Vocabulary	
climate	la Niña
convection	mountains
el Niño	ocean
equator	Poles
Gulf Stream	weather
heat capacity	wind

Use the terms in the vocabulary box to fill in the blanks. Each term may be used as often as needed. You will not need to use all the terms.

1. _____ is the state of the atmosphere at a given time. It includes features such as temperature, wind, air pressure, and moisture.

2. _____ is all the features of the weather for a certain region averaged over a long time.

3. The Sun's heat is most intense at the _____. The Sun's heat becomes less intense as you go toward the _____.

4. Warm ocean currents start near the _____. These currents affect weather and climate by giving off their heat to the air.

5. Water has a high _____, which means that it takes a long time to heat up and to cool down.

6. One way that warm ocean water affects weather and climate is by transferring its heat to the air above the ocean surface. This happens mainly by a process called _____, which transfers heat by forming currents of rising heated material and sinking cooler material in the fluid.

7. The _____ is a warm current that flows north from the equator and along the east coast of North America to Canada.

8. In a similar way, warm currents off the coast of British Columbia bring warm, moist air to the province. The _____ on the coast prevent this air from reaching the interior of British Columbia.

9. _____ is a period during which upwelling causes unusually cold water to rise to the surface off the coast of South America near the equator.

Use textbook pages 428–434.

Oceans, weather, and climate

Answer the questions below.

1. What does it mean to say, "Water has a high heat capacity"?

_____

_____

2. What is weather?

_____

_____

3. What is climate?

_____

_____

4. What does convection do?

_____

_____

5. How does the Gulf Stream affect the climate of the British Isles and northern Europe?

_____

_____

6. What prevents moist ocean air from reaching the interior of British Columbia?

_____

_____

7. What is el Niño?

_____

_____

_____

8. What is la Niña?

_____

_____

_____

Use textbook page 432.

Convection transfers heat

Ocean temperatures can noticeably affect the climate of coastal area.

This diagram represents the rain shadow for British Columbia. Examine the diagrams, and then answer the questions below.

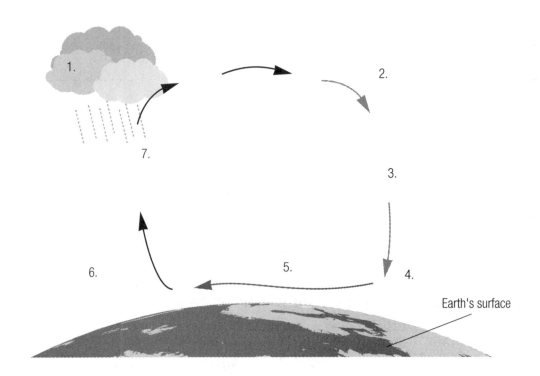

Match each stage of convection to its descriptor. You can use the descriptors as often as necessary.	
Stage of convection	**Descriptor**
_____ 1.	**A.** Air flows from high to low pressure and picks up heat and moisture.
_____ 2.	**B.** Cool, dry air sinks and warms.
_____ 3.	**C.** high pressure
_____ 4.	**D.** low pressure
_____ 5.	**E.** Warm, moist air rises and cools.
_____ 6.	
_____ 7.	

se textbook pages 428–435.

Oceans and climate

Match each Term on the left with the best Descriptor on the right. Each Descriptor may be used only once.

Term	Descriptor
1. _____ climate	A. a warm ocean current that develops every few years
2. _____ convection	B. the process of heat transfer through the flow of a heated fluid
3. _____ el Niño	
4. _____ heat capacity	C. state of the atmosphere at a given time
5. _____ la Niña	D. the weather characteristics of a region averaged over a long time
6. _____ weather	E. a measure of how long it takes for a material to heat up or cool down
	F. wind currents that start near the equator
	G. colder than normal water coming to the surface due to upwelling

Circle the letter of the best answer.

7. If you say "Winters are mild where I live," what are you describing?

A. weather

B. climate

C. convection

D. heat capacity

8. If you say "It's going to rain all day tomorrow," what are you describing?

A. weather

B. climate

C. convection

D. heat capacity

9. Due to water's heat capacity

A. oceans can store a great deal of heat

B. oceans cannot store heat

C. oceans can get very cold

D. oceans can get very hot

10. What is one way that oceans affect weather and climate?

A. by depositing sediment to make beaches

B. by transferring heat to the air

C. by taking a short time to cool down

D. by taking a short time to heat up

11. Which of the following correctly describes the Gulf Stream?

A. a cold current of water from the Arctic

B. a warm current of water from the British Isles

C. a current that flows north from the equator along the east coast of North America.

D. the current that brings warm, moist air to the coast of British Columbia

12. In an el Niño year

A. there are warmer than usual surface water temperatures in the western Pacific Ocean

B. there are warmer than usual surface water temperatures in the eastern Pacific Ocean

C. unusually cold water rises to the surface of the eastern Pacific Ocean

D. unusually cold water rises to the surface of the western Pacific Ocean

Freshwater Environments

Textbook pages 440–447

Before You Read

What types of plants and animals live in freshwater environments? Write your ideas on the lines below. Then read on to find out about freshwater environments.

 **Mark the Text**

Identify Details

As you read the section, use one colour to highlight the text that describes freshwater environments. Use another colour to highlight other facts about the plants and animals that live there.

What are freshwater environments?

Freshwater environments include lakes, ponds, wetlands, rivers, streams, and estuaries. All of these environments contain fresh water, rather than the salt water that is found in oceans. All of these environments support a wide variety of living things.

Several factors determine the forms of life that live in freshwater environments. These factors include:

◆ how far down into the water sunlight reaches

◆ the amount of nutrients

◆ the depth of the water

◆ how fast the water moves

◆ how much oxygen is in the water

What are lakes and ponds like?

Lakes and ponds are large holes in the ground that hold water. Lakes are larger than ponds. In a pond, sunlight can reach all the way to the bottom. In a lake, sunlight does not reach the bottom, except near the shoreline.

Plants in lakes and ponds grow wherever sunlight can reach. Along the edges of lakes and ponds, common plants include rushes, cattails, and water lilies. Farther from shore, tiny plant-like living things called phytoplankton use the Sun's energy to make food for themselves. Tiny animals and animal-like living things called zooplankton feed on the phytoplankton. Both phytoplankton and zooplankton are food for fish and birds. ✔

Reading Check

1. What determines where plants grow in ponds and lakes?

_____

_____

_____

Name

Date

Section
12.1
Summary

continued

What are wetlands?

Wetlands are places where there is standing water covering the land all or much of the time. Marshes, bogs, and the shores of ponds, lakes, rivers, and streams are types of wetlands. Many kinds of plants grow in these areas.

Wetlands are important for many reasons. For example, wetlands store water, which helps to prevent flooding. The roots of the plants help make the ground more stable. Many kinds of birds and fish breed in these areas. Insects and many other kinds of animals live in or visit wetlands as part of their life cycle.

What are streams and rivers like?

Streams and rivers are fast-moving waterways. In general, the main difference between streams and rivers is size. Streams are smaller than rivers. Individual streams and rivers can vary greatly in speed, temperature, and how clear the water is.

Imagine living in an environment that is always moving. That is what it is like to live in rivers and streams. Fish and other swimming animals easily live in these environments. Other living things attach themselves to rocks on the sides or bottom of the stream or river. Plants grow along the shore. Insects lay their eggs there, too.

What is an estuary?

An **estuary** is an area of moderately salty water where a river flows into an ocean. This type of water is called "brackish." Estuaries are rich in nutrients that come from the rivers and the ocean. These nutrients feed a wide variety of plants, fish, birds, and mammals. ✔

✔ Reading Check

2. Explain why you could find an estuary on the coasts of British Columbia, but not in the interior.

Use with textbook pages 440–446.

Different kinds of freshwater environments

Answer the questions below.

1. Name one similarity and one difference between streams and rivers.

_____

_____

_____

2. What kind of plants live at the edges of lakes and ponds?

_____

_____

_____

_____

3. Explain the differences between phytoplankton and zooplankton.

_____

_____

_____

4. Why are wetlands important to the environment?

_____

_____

_____

_____

5. What makes estuaries ideal for both plants and animals?

_____

_____

_____

_____

Use with textbook pages 440–447.

Fresh water

Vocabulary	
brackish	phytoplankton
depth	ponds
estuaries	rivers
fast	salt
flooding	stable
lakes	streams
nutrients	standing
oceans	sunlight
oxygen	wetlands
	zooplankton

Use the terms in the vocabulary box above to fill in the blanks. Each term may be used as often as needed. You will not need to use all the terms.

1. Six types of freshwater environments are _____,
   _____, _____, _____,
   _____, and_____.

2. Factors that determine the forms of life that live in freshwater environments include:
   • how far down into the water _____ reaches

   • the amount of _____ for plants and animals

   • the _____ of the water (where it is deep or shallow)

   • how _____ the water moves

   • how much _____ is in the water for the plants and animals to
     breathe

3. Tiny plant-like living things called_____ use the Sun's energy to make
   food for themselves.

4. Wetlands are places where there is _____ water covering the land all
   or much of the time.

5. Wetlands store water, which helps to prevent _____. The roots of the
   plants help make the ground more _____.

6. _____ are areas of moderately salty water where a river flows into an
   ocean. This type of water is called _____ water.

Use with textbook pages 441–443.

Living in fresh water

Use words and pictures to describe each of the following freshwater environments. Be sure to draw or describe the movement of the water and the plants and animals that live there.

pond	wetland
river	**estuary**

Use with textbook pages 440–447.

Freshwater environments

Match the Term on the left with the best Descriptor on the right. Each Descriptor may be used only once.

Term	Descriptor
1. _____ brackish	**A.** includes bogs and marshes
2. _____ estuary	**B.** tiny plants and plant-like organisms
3. _____ phytoplankton	**C.** mixture of fresh and salt water
4. _____ wetland	**D.** tiny animals and animal-like organisms
5. _____ zooplankton	**E.** fast-moving waterways
	F. an area of moderately salty water where a river flows into an ocean

Circle the letter of the best answer.

6. Which of the following is not a freshwater environment?

A. wetland

B. estuary

C. tidal pool

D. pond

7. Which factors determine which plants and animals live in a freshwater environment?

I.	how much oxygen is in the water
II.	how fast the water moves
III.	how deep the water is
IV.	how far down the sunlight reaches

A. I and II only

B. I, II, and III only

C. II and III only

D. I, II, III, and IV

8. Which of the following is true of wetlands?

I.	they store water and help prevent flooding
II.	they are home to many kinds of birds and fish
III.	they combine both fresh and salt water
IV.	they include both fast-moving and slow-moving water

A. I and II only

B. I, II, and III only

C. II and III only

D. I, II, III, and IV

9. Which of the following is correct?

A. zooplankton are tiny plant-like organisms

B. zooplankton produce food from sunlight

C. phytoplankton are eaten by fish

D. phytoplankton eat zooplankton

10. Which environment does the following statement describe? "Fish and other swimming animals easily live in these fast-moving environments."

A. wetlands

B. estuaries

C. rivers

D. lakes

11. Which of the following is true of estuaries?

A. it is difficult for plants and animals to live there

B. there are few nutrients

C. they are formed where the ocean flows into a river

D. they are a mixture of salt water and fresh water

Saltwater Environments

Textbook pages 448–453

Before You Read

What kinds of living things live near the surface of the ocean? What kinds of living things live near the bottom of the ocean? Record your ideas on the lines below.

 **Mark the Text**

Identify Concepts
Highlight each question head in this section. Then use a different colour to highlight the answers to the questions.

✔ *Reading Check*

1. What is the pelagic zone?

_____

_____

_____

✔ *Reading Check*

2. What is the benthic zone?

_____

_____

_____

What lives in the ocean?

There are living things throughout the ocean. They range in size from single cells to huge animals, such as the blue whale. There are tiny phytoplankton and zooplankton, plants, fish, and mammals. There are other kinds of animals, too, such as clams, squids, and sponges. All the life in the ocean is found in one of two large regions. These are called the pelagic zone and the benthic zone.

What is the pelagic zone?

The **pelagic zone** includes the ocean water to a depth of 4000 m. Nearly 90 percent of all living things in the ocean live within the first 200 m because this is the average depth to which sunlight can reach in the ocean. Plants and plant-like living things can only grow in the part of the water where sunlight can reach. The pelagic zone is divided into three zones, the sunlight, twilight, and midnight zones. These zones are outlined in the table on the next page. ✔

What is the benthic zone?

The cold, dark part of the ocean that is deeper than 4000 m from the surface is called the **benthic zone**. It reaches down to the bottom of the ocean. Even at these depths there is life. Plants do not grow in the deep darkness of the benthic zone. So the living things in this zone use food other than plants to survive. ✔

Because there is no sunlight in the benthic zone, some living things make their own light. They can use chemical reactions in their bodies to make some of their body parts glow to help them find food, attract a mate, or scare away enemies.

© 2006 McGraw-Hill Ryerson Limited

Name

Date

Section
12.2
Summary

continued

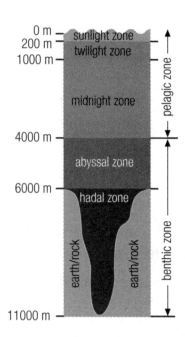

Zones of the Ocean

Zone	Depth	Description
pelagic		
sunlight (epipelagic)	0–200 m	Sunlight penetrates this zone, allowing photosynthesis in plants.
twilight	200–1000 m	The light reaching this zone is very dim and will not allow plants to grow.
midnight (bathypelagic)	1000–4000 m	No light reaches this zone.
benthic		
abyssal	4000–6000 m	This is the zone at the bottom of the ocean. Temperatures are freezing cold and water pressure is enormous.
hadal	greater than 6000 m	This zone is found in the deepest ocean trenches.

Use with textbook pages 448–450.

Living in saltwater

Vocabulary	
20 m	light
200 m	midnight
abyssal	pelagic
benthic	sunlight
food	twilight
hadal	

Use the terms in the vocabulary box to fill in the blanks. Each term may be used as often as needed. You will not need to use all the terms.

1. All the life in the ocean is found in one of two large regions. These are called the _____ zone and the _____ zone.

2. The _____ zone includes the ocean water to a depth of 4000 m.

3. Nearly 90 percent of all living things in the ocean live within the first _____ because this is the average depth to which sunlight can reach in the ocean.

4. The pelagic zone is divided into three zones, the _____, _____, and _____ zones.

5. Sunlight penetrates the _____ zone, allowing plants to make their own food.

6. The light reaching the _____ zone is very dim and will not allow plants to grow.

7. The cold, dark part of the ocean that is deeper than 4000 m from the surface is called the _____ zone.

8. The benthic zone is divided into two zones, the _____ zone and the _____ zone.

9. The _____ zone is at the bottom of the ocean. Temperatures are freezing cold and water pressure is enormous.

10. The _____ zone is found in the deepest ocean trenches.

11. Because there is no sunlight in the benthic zone, some living things make their own _____ using chemical reactions in their bodies.

Use with textbook page 448.

Ocean water environments

Label the zones of ocean water. Describe the environment of each zone.

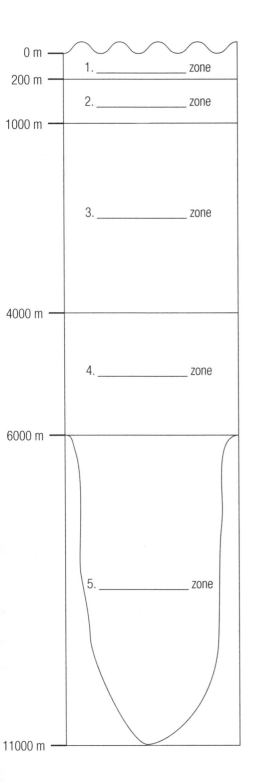

Description

1. _____
   _____
   _____
   _____

2. _____
   _____
   _____

3. _____
   _____
   _____

4. _____
   _____
   _____

5. _____
   _____
   _____

Use with textbook page 450.

Food webs

Study the diagram below of a food web of the Pacific Ocean. The arrows show what
food is eaten by what creatures. For example, the arrows show that the baleen whale eats
zooplankton, and zooplankton eat phytoplankton.

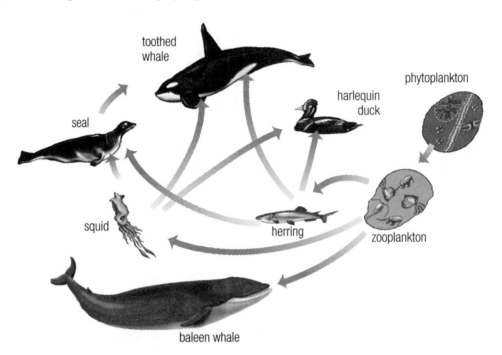

**Use the food web to help you complete the following food chains. Some answers are
provided to help you.**

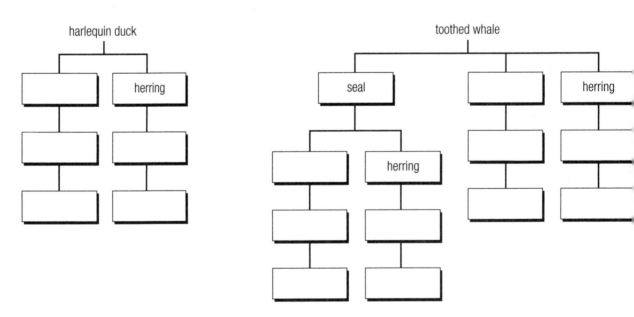

Use with textbook pages 448–453.

Saltwater environments

Match the Term on the left with the best Descriptor on the right. Each Descriptor may be used only once.	
Term	**Descriptor**
1. _____ midnight zone **2.** _____ benthic zone **3.** _____ sunlight zone **4.** _____ hadal zone **5.** _____ pelagic zone	**A.** zone where sunlight reaches **B.** zone between 1000 m and 4000 m **C.** zone at the bottom of the ocean between 4000 m and 6000 m **D.** open water between zero and 4000 m **E.** between 4000 m and 11 000 m **G.** found in the deepest ocean trenches

Circle the letter of the best answer.

6. The pelagic zone can be divided into

A. the sunlight zone, twilight zone, and hadal zone

B. the midnight zone, twilight zone, and abyssal zone

C. the twilight zone, abyssal zone, and hadal zone

D. sunlight zone, twilight zone, and midnight zone

7. Almost 90 percent of all sea creatures live

A. on the bottom of the ocean

B. near the surface of the ocean

C. in the middle of the ocean

D. between the middle and the bottom of the ocean

8. The benthic zone can be divided into

A. the sunlight zone, twilight zone, and hadal zone

B. the midnight zone and abyssal zone

C. the abyssal zone and hadal zone

D. sunlight zone, twilight zone, and midnight zone

9. The abyssal zone is found

A. between 0 m and 200 m

B. between 200 m and 1000 m

C. between 1000 m and 4000 m

D. between 4000 m and 6000 m

10. Why do some living things in the benthic zone make their own light?

I.	to find food
II.	to attract a mate
III.	to make food
IV.	to scare away enemies

A. I and II only

B. III only

C. I, II, and IV only

D. I, II, III, and IV

11. Why do plants not grow in the benthic zone?

A. There is no sunlight.

B. The water is too cold.

C. There are not enough nutrients.

D. There is no oxygen.

Water Quality and Its Effects on Living Things

Textbook pages 454–463

Before You Read

All living things need water to survive. Harmful substances that are released into the environment can pollute water. What examples of water pollution can you think of? Write your thoughts on the lines below.

_____

_____

Create a Quiz

After you have read this section, create five questions based on what you have learned. After you write the questions, be sure to answer them.

 **Reading Check**

1. Name one point source of water pollution and one non-point source.

_____

_____

_____

What are sources of water pollution?

Point sources of water pollution are sources that directly pollute the water. For instance, an oil spill is a point source of pollution. So is dumping garbage from a boat or dock. In each example there is one source of pollution.

Non-point sources of water pollution are sources that indirectly pollute the water. There is more than one source. For instance, think of someone putting pesticide (poison) on a lawn or field. When it rains, some of the pesticide can get washed into the soil and be absorbed. The pesticide may find its way into ground water. And the ground water may feed into a stream or river. The stream or river then carries the pesticide into a lake or an ocean. ✓

What effects does water pollution have?

Harmful chemicals in water can hurt or kill things that live in water. These chemicals also can harm or kill people and other living things that drink polluted water. Animals (including people) may eat other living things that are sick or poisoned from pollution. They can become sick themselves.

Other kinds of pollutants, such as old fishing nets and plastic rings, can hurt living things if they get tangled in them. Oil spills hurt and kill living things because the oil sticks to them. They may suffocate because they cannot breathe. Birds cannot fly with oil on their wings.

ow does pollution in the air affect water quality?

Some pollutants are gases and particles that are given off by cars, trucks, and smokestacks. The wind carries these pollutants high into the air. They mix and dissolve with water vapour, and they form strong acids. The **acidic precipitation** (acid rain and acid snow) that carries this acidic water back to Earth makes water in ponds and lakes more acidic than they normally are. Precipitation is called acidic if it has a pH of less than 5.0. (pH is a measure of how acidic or basic a substance is.) ✓

Pollutants that are given off into the air also include heavy metals, such as lead and mercury. These, too, can mix with water vapour. Rain returns these toxic substances to water systems on Earth.

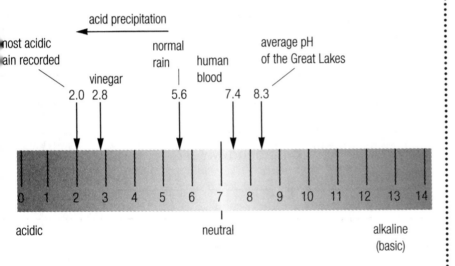

Reading Check

2. What is acidic precipitation?

_____

_____

_____

Use with textbook pages 454–460.

Water quality

Every organism on Earth needs water to survive. Many factors can affect water quality.

Answer the questions below about water quality.

1. What is pollution?

_____

_____

_____

2. What are point sources of pollution?

_____

_____

_____

3. What are non-point sources of pollution?

_____

_____

_____

4. What effect does non-point pollution have on ground water?

_____

_____

_____

_____

5. How is acidic precipitation formed?

_____

_____

_____

_____

Use with textbook pages 454–460.

Water pollution

Vocabulary	
5.0	oil spill
7.0	pesticide
acidic precipitation	pH
acidic	point sources
acids	pollutants
non-point sources	pollution
oil	

Use the terms in the vocabulary box above to fill in the blanks. Each term may be used as often as needed. You will not need to use all the terms.

1. _____ of water pollution are sources that directly pollute the water.

2. A(n) _____ is a point source of pollution. So is dumping garbage from a boat or dock.

3. _____ of water pollution are sources that indirectly pollute the water.

4. Someone putting _____ (poison) on a lawn or field is a non-point source of pollution.

5. Other kinds of _____, such as old fishing nets and plastic rings, can hurt living things if they get tangled in them.

6. Oil spills hurt and kill living things because the _____ sticks to them.

7. Some _____ are gases and particles that are given off by cars, trucks, and smokestacks. They mix and dissolve with water vapour, and they form strong _____.

8. The _____ that carries this acidic water back to Earth makes water in ponds and lakes more _____ than they normally are.

9. _____ is a measure of how acidic or basic a substance is. Precipitation is called acidic if it has a pH of less than _____.

10. _____ that are given off into the air also include heavy metals such as lead and mercury.

Use with textbook pages 454–460.

Sources of pollution

Draw and describe a point source of water pollution and a non-point source of water pollution.

Point source of pollution

Example:

Non-point source of pollution

Example:

se with textbook pages 454–460.

Water quality and its effects on living things

Match the Term on the left with the best Descriptor on the right. Each Descriptor may be used only once.

Term	Descriptor
1. _____ acid precipitation	A. pollution that is caused indirectly
2. _____ non-point source	B. precipitation with a pH of more than 5.0
3. _____ point source	C. precipitation with a pH of less than 5.0
4. _____ pollution	D. any type of harmful material that is released into the environment
	E. pollution that is caused directly

Circle the letter of the best answer.

5. Pollutants include heavy metals such as

A. lead and mercury

B. fishing nets and plastic rings

C. oil spills and garbage dumps

D. pesticides and chemicals

6. Which of the following is **not** true of acid precipitation?

A. it makes water in ponds and lakes more acidic than normal

B. it is formed when pollutants are dissolved in water vapour

C. it is formed from pollutants given off by smokestacks

D. it is formed when rain dissolves chemicals on the ground

7. How do oil spills affect living things?

A. the living things may suffocate because they cannot breathe

B. birds cannot fly with oil on their wings

C. animals that drink the polluted water might die

D. all of the above

8. Which of the following are point sources of pollution?

I.	gas leaking from a pipe into a stream
II.	someone tossing a plastic water bottle into a lake
III.	someone dumping an oil can into a pond
IV.	gas spilling into the lake when adding gas to the tank of a motorboat

A. II and III only

B. I and IV only

C. I, III, and IV only

D. I, II, III, and IV

9. Which of the following are non-point sources of pollution?

I.	pesticide sprayed from an airplane
II.	fertilizers on lawns and farms
III.	cars and trucks driving along a highway
IV.	smokestacks adding pollutants into the air

A. II and III only

B. I and IV only

C. I, III, and IV only

D. I, II, III, and IV

Notes